EP Language Arts 1

Parent's Guide

Welcome to the EP Language Arts 1 Parent's Guide!

This book was created to help you go offline while following EP's Language Arts 1 curriculum. You will need the Language Arts 1 student workbook for your child. Without the online lessons, you will need to be your child's teacher. The directions are here for introducing new topics. The workbook will provide practice and review.

This book also includes objectives for each day, materials marked where needed, directions for what to do each day, and the complete answer key. The answers can be found at the end of the book.

I've made some headings showing what is covered in sections, but I also wanted to note that handwriting/writing/grammar/spelling is throughout. Every piece of copywork is working on those things as they form the words of well-written sentences.

And a little note: To avoid calling all children "he" or the awkward phrasing of "him or her," I've used the plural pronoun when referring to your child, such as, "Brainstorm with your child words that rhyme with tree, and see how many they can come up with."

Have a great year.

Lee

P.S. There are pictures used in the first two weeks. If you want to see them in color, go to the online Language Arts 1 course on allinonehomeschool.com.

Note: We used to call each lesson a day: "Day 1," "Day 2," etc. We've replaced those days with "lessons," but you'll see "day" still in the mini pages in the answer section. Those pages are the same, not outdated, just that one word is changed.

Spelling/phonics

Lesson 1

- Students will: identify and write rhyming words with the long A sound
- What do you see happening in the picture?

- Read the accompanying poem, *Abroad*.

> Then at the Folkstone harbor, down they go
> Across the gangway to the boat below;
> Mabel and Rose just crossing you can see,
> Each holding her new doll most carefully.
>
> Nellie, Miss Earle, and Bertie too appear,
> Whilst Dennis, with the rugs, brings up the rear.
> May looks behind her with an anxious air,
> Lest Father, at the last, should not be there.

Our children once on board, all safe and sound,
Watch with delight the busy scene around.
The noisy steam-pipe blows and blows away, -
"Now this is just the noise we like," they say.

But while the turmoil loud and louder grows,
"I'm glad the wind blows gently," whispers Rose.
And as the steamer swiftly leaves the quay,
Mabel and Dennis almost dance with glee.

- Ask your child what happened during the poem.
  - o It appears a family is going on some sea voyage.
- Ask your child to listen for the rhyming words at the end of each of the first two lines. Read the first two lines again.
  - o GO rhymes with BELOW.
- Read the poem again and ask your child to listen for rhyming A sound words. For example, the word DAY has an A sound. We call it the long A sound. Ask your child for words that rhyme with DAY.
  - o say, play, may, bay, …
  - o Tell your child to stop you when they hear the two rhyming long A sound words.
    - ▪ away and say
- Lesson 1 worksheet
  - o They will be writing rhyming words. Give them the hint to cross off each word that they use to help them find what words are still left over.

Lesson 2

- Students will: identify rhyming words, write words with the long A sound
- Have your child look at the picture included further into the lesson. What do they see in the picture? What do they think is happening? Let them know this is a continuation of the same story.
- Read the poem to your child.

The sea is calm, and clear the sky – only a few clouds scudding by:
The Passengers look bright, and say, "Are we not lucky in the day!"

The Mate stands in the wheelhouse there, and turns the wheel with watchful care:
Steering to-day is work enough; what must it be when weather's rough?

Look at him in his sheltered place – he hasn't got a merry face –
'Tis not such fun for him, you know, he goes so often to and fro.

Nellie and Father, looking back, glance at the vessel's lengthening track –
"How far," says Nellie, "we have come! good-bye, good-bye, dear English home!"

Dennis and Rose and Mabel, walking upon the deck, are gaily talking –
Says Mabel, "No one must forget to call my new doll 'Antoinette';

Traveling in France, 'twould be a shame for her to have an English name."
Says Dennis, "Call her what you will, so you be English 'Mabel' still.

Says Rose, to Dennis drawing nigher, "I think the wind is getting higher;"
"If a gale blows, do you suppose, we shall be wrecked?" asks little Rose.

- Ask your child, "What is happening? Where did they come from? Where are they going?"
    - It says good-bye dear English home. They are leaving England.
    - The girl gives her doll a French name because they will be traveling in France. So, they are going to France.

- This was another rhyming poem. Have your child listen again for long A sound rhyming words. Have your child stop you when they hear it.
  - say/day, at the very beginning
  - If you want to go on, there are harder ones. place/face, shame/name
- Lesson 2 worksheet
  - They will be filling in the blanks with long A words from the word box. There is also a sentence to copy.

Lesson 3

- Students will: identify words with the long E sound
- Have your child take a look at the picture. What do they see? What do they think is happening? This is a continuation of the same story of their travels.

- Read the poem to your child.

> Here they see a pretty sight,
> Sunny sky and landscape bright:
> Fishing boats move up and down,
> With their sails all red and brown.
>
> Some to land are drawing near,
> O'er the water still and clear,
> Full of fish as they can be,
> Caught last night in open sea.
>
> On the pavement down below,
> Fishwives hurry to and fro,
> Calling out their fish to sell –
> "What a noisy lot," says Nell,
>
> "What a clap – clap – clap – they make
> With their shoes each step they take.
> Wooden shoes, I do declare,
> And oh! what funny caps they wear!"
>
> After breakfast all went out
> To view the streets, and walk about
> The ancient city-walls, so strong,
> Where waved the English flag for long.
>
> Toy shops too they went to see,
> Spread with toys so temptingly;
> Dolls of every kind were there,
> With eyes that shut and real hair –
>
> And, in a brightly-coloured row,
> Doll-fisherfolk like these below.
> Prices marked, as if to say,
> "Come and buy us, quick, to-day!"
>
> One for Mabel, one for Rose,
> *Two* for Bertie I suppose,
> Father bought. – Then all once more
> Set off travelling as before.

- Ask your child what was happening.
    - They are in France now and things are different. They are taking in the new sounds like the wooden shoes clapping on the roads, and the new sights, like the hats that look funny to them.

- o They stop at a toy store but then have to keep on traveling.
- This was another rhyming poem. Ask your child to listen for two long E sound rhyming words.
  - o An example of a long E sound word is the word ME. Ask your child for words that rhyme with me.
    - ▪ bee, tree, see, knee, …
- Have your child stop you when they hear two rhyming words with an E sound.
  - o near/clear, be/sea, see/temptingly
  - o That's the order they appear. They can find any. It's okay if they miss near/clear and catch be/see.
- Lesson 3 worksheet
  - o They will be circling words with the long E sound and then finding those things in the picture.

Lesson 4

- Students will: identify rhyming words, write words with the long E sound
- Have your child look at the picture for this lesson. What do they see in the picture? What do they think is happening? This is still a continuation. All the poems are talking about what they kids experienced in their travels.

- Read the poem to your child.

> Now that dinner is ordered, we'll just take a peep
> At the cooks in the kitchen – just see! what a heap
> Of plates are provided, and copper pots too; -
> They'll soon make a dinner for me and for you.
> French cookery's famous for flavouring rare,
> But of *garlic* I think they've enough and to spare.

If we ask how their wonderful dishes are made,
I'm afraid they won't tell us the tricks of the trade.
Do they make them, I wonder, of frogs and of snails?
Or are these, after all, only travellers' tales?
The names are all down on the "Menu," no doubt,
But the worst of it is that we can't make them out.

- Ask your child what the poem was talking about.
  - They are in France at a restaurant. They talk about the flavors and wonder what's in the food. Could it be a frog or a snail? They can't make out the menus. Can you figure out why?
    - They are in French!
- This was another rhyming poem. Read it again and have your child listen for long-E rhyming words and to stop you when they hear them.
  - peep/heap
- Lesson 4 worksheet
  - They will be finding words with a long E sound and then writing them in the blanks provided.
  - There is also a sentence for copying.

Lesson 5

- Students will: identify rhyming words, write words with the long I sound, sequence a story
- Have your child look at the picture at the end of the lesson. Ask them what they see in the picture and then what they think is happening in the picture.
- Read the poem to your child.

> Here the children came next morn,
> Walking by the river Orne;
> Near the poplars on the green,
> Where the Washerwives are seen,
> Here they looked at old Nannette,
> Wringing out the garments wet;
> Saw how Eugenie, her daughter,
> Soaked them first in running water;
> Watched the washers soaping, scrubbing,
> With their mallets rubbing, drubbing –
> Working hard with all their might,
> Till clothes were clean and white.

- Ask your child what was happening in the poem.
  - There are women out washing clothes. That's how it was done, outside using tubs and running water.
- This, of course, was another rhyming poem. Have your child stop you when you read it again when they hear two long I sound words that rhyme.
  - might/white

- Lesson 5 worksheet
  - They will be filling in blanks in the story with the long I words found in the word box. Then they will order the pictures showing the order they appeared in the story.

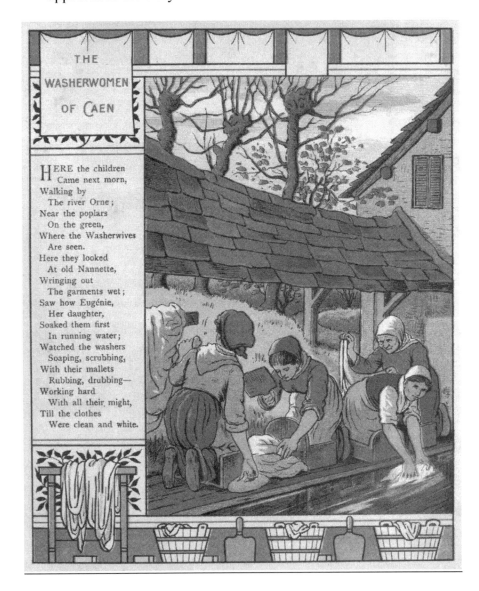

THE WASHERWOMEN OF CAEN

HERE the children
  Came next morn,
Walking by
  The river Orne;
Near the poplars
  On the green,
Where the Washerwives
  Are seen.
Here they looked
  At old Nannette,
Wringing out
  The garments wet;
Saw how Eugénie,
  Her daughter,
Soaked them first
  In running water;
Watched the washers
  Soaping, scrubbing,
With their mallets
  Rubbing, drubbing—
Working hard
  With all their might,
Till the clothes
  Were clean and white.

Lesson 6 (scissors, glue stick)

- Students will: identify rhyming words, identify words with the long I sound
- Look at the picture following. Ask your child what is in the picture and what is happening.
- Read the poem to your child and ask what is happening in the poem.

8

Chocolate and Milk

Little Lili, whose age isn't three years quite,
Went one day with Mamma for a long country walk,
Keeping up, all the time, such a chatter and talk
Of the trees, and the flowers, and the cows, brown and white.

Soon she asked for some cake, and some chocolate too,
For this was her favourite lunch every day –
"Dear child," said Mamma, "let me see – I dare say
If I ask that nice milkmaid, and say it's for you,

Some sweet milk can we get from her pretty cow."
I would rather have chocolate," Lili averred.
Then Mamma said, "Dear Lili, please don't be absurd;
My darling, you cannot have chocolate now:

You know we can't get it so far from the town. –
Come and stroke the white cow, - see, her coat's soft as silk."
"But, Mamma," Lili said, "if the White cow gives milk,
Then chocolate surely must come from the Brown."

- This was another rhyming poem. Have your child listen for two long I sound words. It's trickier because the rhyming lines are not next to each other.
    o quite/white
- Lesson 6 worksheet
    o This is a cut and paste activity. They will be looking for long I sound words

Lesson 7 (crayon)
- Students will: identify rhyming words, identify words with the long O sound
- Look at the picture following. Ask your child what is in the picture and what they think is happening in the picture. Where are they?

- Now read the poem to your child.

> Mumbo and Jumbo, two elephants great,
> From India travelled, and lived in state,
> In Paris the one, and in London the other:
> Now Mumbo and Jumbo were sister and brother.
> A warm invitation to Jumbo came,
> To cross the Atlantic and spread his fame.
> Said he, "I really don't want to go –
> But then, they're so pressing! – I can't say No!"
>
> So away to America Jumbo went,
> But his sister Mumbo is quite content
> To stay with the children of Paris, for she
> Is as happy an elephant as could be:
> "I've a capital house, quite large and airy,
> Close by live the Ostrich and Dromedary,
> And we see our young friends every day," said she;
> "Oh, where is the Zoo that would better suit me?"

- This was another rhyming poem. Have your child listen for two long O sound words and stop you when they hear it.
  - go/no
  - Think together of other words with a long O sound such as boat and road.

- Mumbo and Jumbo were real elephants. Jumbo was sold to America and made famous by P.T. Barnum (of Barnum and Bailey circus). It's where we get our word jumbo, meaning really big.
- Lesson 7 worksheet
  - They will be finding words with a long O sound and coloring in the triangle or square that it's in. If they are correct, they should make a picture.
  - There is also a sentence for copying.

Lesson 8

- Students will: identify rhyming words, write words with the long O sound
- Look at the picture with your child and have your child say what they see and what they think is happening.
  - It's a small train being pulled by a horse.

- Read the poem to your child and have them say what it's talking about.
  - There are some things in here that need explaining. Mumbo is the elephant, who is slow. She couldn't go "steeple-chasing" or horse racing.
  - Conveyances are means of transport.
  - The tramway is the little train in the picture.
  - The Bois (rhymes with bra) and maillot (my-yo) are French.

  A steady steed is Mumbo, if just a trifle slow;
  Upon her back you couldn't well a-steeple-chasing go:
  But other opportunities there are to have a ride,
  For there's a stud of ponies, and a camel to bestride –
  A cart that's drawn by oxen can accommodate a few,

And if such queer conveyances don't please you at the Zoo,
There are little tramway cars too, with seats on either side,
Which will take you through the gardens, and through the Bois beside. –
Take the ticket on the other page, and with it you may go
From the lake within the garden to the gate that's called Maillot.

- This was another rhyming poem. Read it again and have your child stop you when you get to rhyming O words.
  - slow, go
- Lesson 8 worksheet
  - Your child will be writing the words from the word box onto the lines.
  - There is also a sentence for copywork.

Lesson 9

- Students will: identify rhyming words, write words with a long U sound
- Look at the picture for this lesson. Ask your child what they see and that they think is happening.

- Read the poem to your child and ask them what they think it was saying.

  THE SWANS.

  "Ho! pretty swans, do you know, in our Zoo
  The swans of old England are just like you?
  "Don't tell me!" said a cross old bird;
  "I know better, the thing's quite absurd.
  "Their figures, I'm sure, are not worth a glance:
  If you want to see style, you must come to France.
  With a scornful whisk the swan turned tail,
  Spread its wings to the breeze, and was off full-sail.
  "Ho! pretty swan, do you know, in our zoo
  The swans are not half so conceited as you?"

- Think together of words with the long U sound such as blue and new.
- Read the poem again and ask your child to stop you when they hear two words with a long U sound that rhyme.
  - zoo/you
- Lesson 9 worksheet
  - Your child will use the words in the word box to fill in the blanks.
  - There is also a sentence for copying.

Lesson 10 (crayons)

- Students will: identify rhyming words and words with the long U sound, create poetry
- Have your child look at the picture for the lesson and say what they see and what they think is happening.

- Read the poem to your child and have them tell you what's happening.

HOMEWARD BOUND

Hurrah! we're afloat, and away speeds the boat as fast as its paddles can go,
With the wind on its back, and a broad foaming track behind it, as white as the snow.
On board, every eye is strained to descry the white cliffs of our own native land,
And brightly they gleam, as onward we steam, till at length they are close at hand.
The sun shines with glee on the rippling sea, and the pennant strung high on the mast.
But at length it sinks down behind the grey town, and tells us the day is nigh past.
See, there is the port, and near it a fort, and the strong old Castle of Dover –
We're close to the shore – just five minutes more, and the Channel Crossing is over.
Then all safe and sound upon English ground, we bid farewell to the sea –
Jump into the train and start off again as fast as the engine can flee.
We run up to town, and thence travel down to the home in the country, at night;
Then I'm sorry to say, dear Nellie and May, Rose, Dennis and Bertie bright,
We must leave in their home till next holidays come, when, let us hope, it may chance
That our trip will, next Spring, be as pleasant a thing as our swallow flight over to France.

- This is our last poem. They don't need to listen for a rhyme today. They will be writing a rhyme though.
- Lesson 10 worksheet
  - They will be coloring in words with the long U sound such as blue and new.
  - Then they will write two lines of a poem that use two words from the worksheet as their words that rhyme on the end of each line. (They can use a different long U rhyming word if they have an idea.)
    - Example: The wind it came and fiercely blew — whirled the leaves, stirred them like stew.
    - Of course, theirs could be like "I like blue. So do you."

Lesson 11

- Students will: practice their name, phone number, address
- Role play with your child. Greet each other. Say hello. Ask each other your name and share your full name. Ask how they are and tell them it's nice to meet them.
- Lesson 11 worksheet
  - Your child will write their full name (first and last), phone number and address.
  - There is also a sentence for copying.

14

Sequencing Stories – Spelling/Phonics

Lesson 12 (scissors)

- Students will: identify the sequence of a story
- Read the story of *The Boy Who Cried Wolf* to your child. This version was written by Tina Rutherford.

Once there was a boy whose family helped take care of the village sheep. One day, the boy's father told him it was his turn to watch the sheep. He needed to stay with the sheep all night. If a wolf came during the night, all he needed to do was yell, "WOLF!" and the villagers would come help him fight the wolf away and keep the sheep safe.

The boy went out that night excited to help keep the village sheep safe. He wanted to do the best that he could do. The boy decided the villagers needed to practice a wolf drill. He wanted to be sure they were ready to help him if a wolf came. So he decided to yell, "WOLF!" even though there was no danger. Of course, all of the villagers came running. "Where is the wolf?" they asked. "We will fight him away!"

"There is no wolf," the boy replied. "It was just a wolf drill."

"A wolf drill?" they all murmured, walking back to their homes.

The boy's father told his son not to have any more drills. "The villagers know what to do, son. They don't need a drill. Don't call for help unless you really need it."

The boy went back to his job of guarding the sheep, a little hurt that his wolf drill idea hadn't been better received. As he looked up over the flock, he thought he saw the shadow of a wolf. "WOLF!" he yelled immediately.

Once again, the villagers came running. "Where is the wolf?" they asked. "We will fight him away!"

"Over there!" the boy replied. "I saw his shadow."

The villagers searched and searched, but never found a wolf. "It's just the shadow of a bush," they told him. Wearily, they once again returned to their homes.

Hours passed and the boy diligently kept watch over the sheep. Suddenly, he saw a creature sneaking in from the trees. He waited until he was sure, but it most definitely was a wolf. "WOLF!" the boy shouted, and waited for help to arrive. As the wolf crept closer to the flock, no villagers emerged from their homes. "WOLF! WOLF! WOLF!" he tried again. But no one came. The boy's false alarms had led them to believe he was once again calling for help when no help was needed. The wolf got away with one of the sheep that night, and the boy learned a hard lesson about his responsibility as a shepherd.

- Lesson 12 worksheet
    - Cut out the blocks and order them in the order of what happened in the story.

Lesson 13

- Students will: practice spelling words in the AN family
- Lesson 13 worksheet
    - They will copy the words and then draw a line to match them to the pictures.
    - There is a sentence to copy.

Lesson 14

- Students will: find their spelling words
- Lesson 14 worksheet
    - They will find the words from Lesson 13 in a word search puzzle. If they aren't sure of a word, they can turn back the page to see the words written.
    - There is also a sentence to copy.

Lesson 15 (scissors)

- Students will: identify the sequence of a story
- Have your child copy the sentence on the Lesson 15 worksheet page.
- Read the story of *Goldilocks and the Three Bears* to your child. This was written by Tina Rutherford and is printed with her permission.

Once there was a little girl with long, golden curls. Her name was Goldilocks. She was playing near her home one day when she saw a beautiful bird. When it started to fly away, Goldilocks followed it into the forest. After several minutes, it landed on a perch outside of a cute little cottage. Finding the door slightly ajar, Goldilocks ventured inside.

"Hello?" she called. But no one answered. Based on the picture hanging above the mantle of the fireplace, Goldilocks determined that a family of three bears lived in the cottage.

She looked around the home and noticed a table with three bowls of cobbler on it. "Just a little taste," she thought to herself. She tasted the first bowl of cobbler, but it was too hot. She tasted the second bowl, but it was too cold. When she tried the third bowl, she found that it was just right. Before she knew it, Goldilocks had eaten it all up!

Moving into the living room, Goldilocks saw three chairs. "I'll just rest a little before I return home," she thought. She sat in the first chair, but it was much too big. She sat in the second chair, but it was too small. She sat in the third chair and found it to be just right. When she started to relax, the chair started to groan and before she knew it, the chair had broken to pieces and deposited her on the floor.

Goldilocks rubbed her bumps and bruises and decided to explore upstairs. She saw a small bedroom with three beds. "That fall really hurt. Maybe I'll lay down for a few minutes," she thought. She crawled into the first bed, but it was too hard. She crawled into the second bed, but it was too soft. She crawled into the third bed and found it to be the most comfortable bed she had ever been in. Only a few moments passed before Goldilocks fell fast asleep.

It wasn't long before the three bears returned home. They had gone for a walk to allow their cobbler to cool, but never expected what they found when they came back. "Someone has been eating my cobbler!" Papa Bear exclaimed. "Someone has been eating my cobbler!" Mama Bear gasped. "Someone has been eating my cobbler, and they ate it all up!" Baby Bear cried.

The bears looked around to find the culprit. Entering the living room, Papa Bear inspected the cushions on his chair. "Hmm. Someone has been sitting in my chair," he proclaimed. "Someone has been sitting in my chair, too," Mama Bear added. "Someone has been sitting in my chair, and they broke it to pieces!" Baby Bear moaned.

Heading upstairs, the three bears entered their bedroom. Noticing the ruffled covers, Papa Bear commented, "Someone has been sleeping in my bed." Mama Bear noticed, "Someone has been sleeping in my bed, too." Baby Bear cried, "Someone has been sleeping in my bed, and here she is!"

Hearing the commotion, Goldilocks began to stir. When she opened her eyes, she found herself face to face with the three bears. She let out a horrified scream and ran out of the house. "I guess she won't be coming here again," Papa Bear commented. "I hope she knows her way home," Mama Bear worried. Baby Bear slumped on the floor and pouted, "I wanted her to stay and play."

- Lesson 15 worksheet
  - Cut out the blocks and have your child order them in the order of what happened in the story.

Lesson 16 (blue and green crayons)

- Students will: identify the sound an S makes at the end of a word
- Lesson 16 worksheet
  - Do the first two with your child. Have your child read the word BUS and the word HAS.
    - BUS ends with the S sound; HAS ends with a Z sound.
  - Have your child read each word out loud to identify which sound the S has at the end of the word.
  - There is a sentence to copy. Remember that each of these is not only handwriting practice, but also a practice in writing not only correct, but well-written sentences.

Lesson 17

- Students will: complete words with consonant blends
- Lesson 17 worksheet
  - Your child will need to read the story and figure out what words go in each blank.
    - You can help your child by showing them how they can attach each ending onto the word to see what makes sense.
    - For instance, the first blank has SLE in it. What makes sense?
      - slenk, slent, slept...
  - There is also a sentence for copying.

Lesson 18

- Students will: identify beginning blend sounds, spell words
- Ask your child what two letters begin the word TRUCK.
  - TR
  - We call these beginning blends.
- Try another. Ask your child what two letters begin the word SNOW.
  - SN
- Lesson 18 worksheet
  - They will just have to write the first beginning blend sounds for each word. Each blend shown in the box is used once.
    - Then they should try to fully spell some of the words, at least two.
    - If any are spelled incorrectly, have them erase their mistake and give them the letters to spell it correctly.
  - There is also a sentence to copy.

Lesson 19

- Students will: identify words beginning and ending with the CH sound
- Ask your child if they can think of any words that begin with the CH sound.
  - child, children, checkers
  - Tell your child that CH is spelled C-H.
- Ask you child if they can think of any words that end with the CH sound.
  - bench, catch, lunch
  - Ask your child how to spell the CH sound.
    - C-H
- Lesson 19 worksheet
  - They will circle and write words that begin and end with the CH sound.
  - There is a sentence to copy as well.

Lesson 20

- Students will: identify and write words that end with CK
- Ask your child to think of words that end with the CK sound.
  - pick, rock, stack
  - Tell your child that all of those end with C-K. That's how we almost always spell words that end with a CK sound.
- Lesson 20 worksheet
  - They will circle the words that end with CK and then find their pictures.
  - They will write CK words and copy a sentence.

Story Writing – Spelling/Phonics

Lesson 21

- Students will: identify the sequence of stories
- Lesson 21 worksheet
  - They will read the three short stories and number the pictures to show the order they come into the story.
  - The last one has a picture of an atom. That represents science.

Lesson 22

- Students will: sequence a story and illustrate a book report
- Choose a story your child is very familiar with or go ahead and read a children's book together.
- Lesson 22 worksheet
  - Have your child think of six things in order that happen in the story.
  - Together write a sentence for each one.
    - You can write these next to the six boxes for Lesson 22 in the workbook.
  - Have your child illustrate the six sentences, drawing pictures in the boxes.

Lesson 23

- Students will: spell words in the OT family
- Ask your child to think of words that rhyme with HOT.
  - pot, lot, rot, shot, trot
- Lesson 23 worksheet
  - They will be copying words that end with OT.
  - Then they will use the picture and their sense of rhyme to figure out what goes on the blank lines. They are all words from the OT family.

Lesson 24

- Students will: practice their OT spelling words
- Lesson 24 worksheet
  - They will be finding the words from Lesson 23 in a word search. If they are unsure of a word, they can turn back the page to see it written.

Lesson 25

- Students will: write correctly ordered sentences
- Lesson 25 worksheet
  - Have your child read the sentence out loud in the correct way before they start writing it down. It should sound right to them.

Lesson 26

- Students will: write correctly ordered sentences
- Lesson 26 worksheet
  - Have your child read the sentence out loud in the correct way before they start writing it down. It should sound right to them.

Lesson 27

- Students will: write about a main character
- Lesson 27 worksheet
  - If writing is physically hard for your child, you could write this for them, so that the writing itself doesn't ruin the thoughtful writing process.
  - If your child has an idea of their own story, by all means write about that character. Otherwise, just have them retell a story they know well.
  - Have your child describe the main character as much as possible. Maybe there is a villain or a best friend that needs to be described as well.
    - For instance, *Finding Nemo*: Marlin is a clown fish. He lost his whole family except for his son, Nemo. He's really careful and worried about everything.

Lesson 28

- Students will: develop the plot of their story
- Lesson 28 worksheet
  - Again, you could write this for your child if the writing will keep them from giving ideas.
  - This time you are going to write what the main character does and then what happens as a result.
  - Lesson 29 will be the conclusion, so we're just talking general things here.
    - For instance, *Finding Nemo*: The father searches across the whole ocean for Nemo and Nemo finds out about it.

Lesson 29

- Students will: write a conclusion
- Lesson 29 worksheet
  - What's the exciting conclusion to your story? What does the main character do and what is the final result?
  - Again, you could write this for your child to keep the handwriting from stopping the writing if that's a problem.
  - Example, *Finding Nemo*: Nemo escapes into the ocean and finds his dad and shows his dad that he doesn't have to worry about him.

Lesson 30

- Students will: read in front of an audience, illustrate their story
- Have your child read the story they put together in front of an audience (could just be you or you could video it or get Grandma or someone online to listen.)
- Lesson 30 worksheet
  - Draw an illustration for your story or a cover for your book.
    - You could take out all the pages with your story on it and staple them into a book.

<u>Beginning and Ending Blends</u>

Lesson 31 (blue, brown, and yellow crayons)

- Students will: identify and write the SH sound at the beginning and end of words
- With your child come up with words that begin with SH sound, like shoes.
  - shop, ship, shy, shampoo, shaping, shaker
- Then come up with words that end with the SH sound like brush.
  - fish, wash, mesh, fresh, wish
- Lesson 31 worksheet
  - They will follow the directions to color in the shapes and reveal a picture.
  - They will copy some of the words in the picture, and there is a sentence to copy as well.
    - Writing words with the same spelling pattern, such as several words with SH is a spelling lesson in writing that sound.

Lesson 32 (scissors, glue stick)

- Students will: differentiate between the hard and soft TH sound, write words with TH
- Practice saying the TH sound together by sticking your tongue out a bit.
  - Ask your child if they can hear the difference in the beginning sound of these two words even though they both start with TH.
    - thing, the

- See if together you can make soft and hard TH sounds.
    o Here are some more pairs using TH, both soft and hard.
        ▪ think, then
        ▪ with, weather
- Encourage your child to read the words out loud to determine if they have a hard or soft TH sound.
- Lesson 32 worksheet
    o You might want to start with writing words and copying the sentence since the page will be cut into.
    o Then the words squares need to be cut out and then glued on to their correct place.

Lesson 33

- Students will: identify and write words that begin with WH
- Lesson 33 worksheet
    o Have your child cross out any words that don't begin with WH.
    o Point out that the remaining words all begin with W-H even though they just have a W sound.
    o They will find the words in the word search puzzle and then copy some of them out on the lines provided.

Lesson 34

- Students will: identify the beginning letters of words beginning with THR and SHR and copy words that begin with those trigraphs
- Ask your child to figure out what the first three letters are of the word THREE.
    o THR
    o Can they think of any other words that start THR?
        ▪ throw, thread
- Ask your child to figure out what the first three letters are of the word SHRIMP.
    o SHR
    o Can they think of any other words that start with SHR?
        ▪ shrink, shrank, shrugged, shrubs
- Lesson 34 worksheet
    o They will write either THR or SHR before each half-completed word. Encourage your child to read the words out loud and try each beginning on them to see which makes sense.
    o Then they will be writing some full words on the lines provided.

Lesson 35

- Students will: identify the silent E that turns short vowels into long vowels
- Write out for your child these words to read. (Or just show them here in the book.)
    o can cane
    o her here

- o fin fine
- o hop hope
- o cub cube
- Ask your child what was added to the second word each time to change the sound of the word?
  - o It's an E. But, we don't say the E. It's silent. It just gives us the clue we need for how to say the word.
  - o When the silent E is there, we use the long vowel sounds. That's when the vowels say their names. A says A. E says E. I says I. O says O. U says U.
- Lesson 35 worksheet
  - o This is a maze they will complete by following the directions telling them which way to turn. To figure it out they will have to decide if the word ends with a silent E or not.
  - o They will also be writing words from the maze with a silent E.

Writing

Lesson 36

- Students will: identify the main idea from a picture
- Lesson 36 worksheet
  - o There are two sentences provided and they will choose the most appropriate one.

Lesson 37 (book)

- Students will: practice ending punctuation
- Introduce periods, exclamation points, and question marks.
  - o Show your child how you can tell a sentence in a book.
    - ▪ Each starts with a capital letter (the big ones) and ends with a punctuation mark.
    - ▪ Show your child a period, exclamation point, and question mark in the book if you can.
  - o Have your child say something boring.
    - ▪ That sentence ended in a period.
  - o Have your child say something super exciting!
    - ▪ That sentence ended in an exclamation point. (If they haven't seen one, you can show your child what it looks like in their workbook on the Lesson 37 page.)
  - o Have your child ask you a question.
    - ▪ That sentence ended in a question mark.
      - • Again, show your child what it looks like if they don't know. It's in their workbook for today.

- Lesson 37 worksheet
  - They will circle which punctuation mark each sentence should end in.
  - There is copywork as well.
    - You can point out that when they copy their sentences carefully, they are practicing writing. Remind your child when they are copying, that every sentence should begin with a capital letter and end with a punctuation mark. In today's sentence there is a name. All names also begin with a capital letter.

Lesson 38

- Students will: learn that the word I is always capitalized
- Ask your child what the first letter in every sentence should look like.
  - uppercase (big)
- Ask your child what the first letter of every name should look like.
  - uppercase (big)
- Tell your child that there is a special word that is always written with an uppercase letter. It's I. Your special name for yourself is always capitalized.
- Lesson 38 worksheet
  - Tell your child that all the sentences have the same mistake. See if they can find what's wrong with the sentences.
    - All of the I's are lowercase.
  - They will be copying the sentences on the page but changing the lowercase I's to uppercase I's.

Lesson 39

- Students will: identify the proper usage of IS/ARE
- Lesson 39 worksheet
  - Encourage your child to read the sentences out loud to see which sounds correct, IS or ARE.

Lesson 40

- Students will: use ARE after plural nouns and IS after singular nouns
- Ask your child which sentence should have IS and which should use ARE.
  - The dog ___ barking.
  - The dogs ____ barking.
    - The dog is barking. The dogs are barking.
    - When there is more than one thing, you use ARE. When there is just one, you use IS.
- Lesson 40 worksheet
  - Your child will write IS or ARE in the blanks. You can encourage your child to read the sentences out loud to hear which sounds correct.
  - There is also a sentence for copying.

Vowel Sounds

Lesson 41 (blue and gray crayons)

- Students will: identify long and short A sounds
- Lesson 41 worksheet
  - They will follow the directions to identify which words have the long A sound. They all have the silent E.
  - Encourage your child to read the words out loud to hear if the A says its name.
  - There is also a sentence to copy. You can point out the exclamation point. Make sure your child is copying carefully. There are quotation marks to copy as well. You can point out to your child that means that whatever is inside the quotes is being said.

Lesson 42

- Students will: identify long and short E sounds
- Lesson 42 worksheet
  - Encourage your child to read each word out loud to see if E says its name.
    - These do not have a silent E. They have EE or EA. The phonics rule for that is that when there are two vowels together, the first one says its name. Starfall says, "When two vowels go a walking, the first does the talking."
  - There is also a sentence to copy on this page.

Lesson 43

- Students will: identify long and short I sounds
- Lesson 43 worksheet
  - They will write in the blanks which word fits the sentence. Each sentence has the choice of a long and short vowel word.

Lesson 44 (scissors and glue)

- Students will: identify long and short O sounds
- Lesson 44 worksheet
  - Have your child do the copywork first.
    - There's a question mark in this one if you want to point it out.
    - There are quotation marks as well. You could ask your child what Benjamin Bat is saying.
    - You can also ask what kind of letter Benjamin starts with since it's a name.
      - capital (big)

- o Then your child can cut out the squares and glue them onto the correct side of the page.
- o These long O sound words all have the silent E to make the O say its name.

Lesson 45

- Students will: identify long and short U sounds
- Lesson 45 worksheet
    - o Your child will be copying the words onto the blanks by deciding which have the long vowel sound where U says its name and which have the short U sound like in hut.
        - ▪ The long U words all have a silent E.
    - o There is also a sentence to copy.
        - ▪ You can ask your child who is saying, "I shall be willing to step outside."
            - • Solomon

Inferences

Lesson 46

- Students will: make inferences
- Read this little story to your child.
    - o There are so many smells in the house, and they are all good. Mom has been in the kitchen since she woke up this morning. There are three pies cooling, and the turkey is about to come out of the oven. I can't wait to eat, especially to make a big pool of gravy in my mashed potatoes!
- Ask your child what day do they think it is?
    - o It's Thanksgiving.
- How do they know that if the story didn't say it?
    - o They made an inference. Sometimes it's called reading between the lines. The story told you by mentioning all the food, especially the turkey.
- Lesson 46 worksheet
    - o Your child will read the sentences on the page and make an inference. Then they will draw a picture to show the time of year they think it is.

Lesson 47

- Students will: write appropriate ending punctuation for sentences
- See if your child remembers how to write a period, exclamation point, and question mark.
- Ask your child when you use a period.
    - o at the end of a normal sentence

- Ask your child when you use an exclamation point
  - at the end of a sentence where you are exclaiming something, maybe shouting it
- Ask your child when you use a question mark.
  - at the end of a question
- Lesson 47 worksheet
  - Your child will decide which punctuation mark each sentence needs.
  - There is also a sentence that needs copying. Make sure they are paying attention to all the details of the sentence.

Lesson 48

- Students will: make an inference
- Lesson 48 worksheet
  - They will read the story and make an inference about what happened. They will show their answer by drawing a picture.

Lesson 49

- Students will: sequence story actions
- Stories have beginnings, middles, and ends. Think of a favorite story and a simple way to describe the beginning, middle, and end.
  - Example: The Hungry Caterpillar is little and hungry, he eats, he turns into a butterfly.
- Lesson 49 worksheet
  - There are three stories on the page. They will decide the beginning, middle, and end of each story by numbering them 1, 2, 3.

Lesson 50

- Students will: write a story that requires the reader to make an inference
- Lesson 50 worksheet
  - Read over the example in the workbook with your child. Brainstorm ideas of what clues they could give the reader that they are talking about a cat.
  - If the physical part of writing is hard for your child, let them dictate their sentences to you.

Phonics/Spelling

Lesson 51

- Students will: identify words with the AR sound
- Tell your child that car is spelled C-A-R.
  - Together make the AR sound, like a pirate!

- Brainstorm words that have the AR sound.
    - farm, barn, tar, etc.
- Lesson 51 worksheet
    - There is a word box and word search on this page.
    - Then they will write some AR words that aren't on the page. Encourage them to try to write the words on their own without you giving them the letters.

Lesson 52

- Students will: practice with ER, UR, IR
- Lesson 52 worksheet
    - Turn to the page in the workbook and read together the letter pairs in the box. They all sound the same.
    - They are going to have to go by what looks right in each word. This should be done in pencil!
    - After they write a word, encourage them to read the sentence and see if the word looks correct.

Lesson 53

- Students will: make inferences, identify words with OR
- Lesson 53 worksheet
    - Your child will find the OR words in the box and in the picture.
    - Your child will choose the best inference from the sentence given.

Lesson 54 (scissors, glue stick)

- Students will: identify and write rhyming words
- Lesson 54 worksheet
    - You might want to do the writing part first before you cut the page. They are going to write words that rhyme with fire.
    - Then they can cut out the tires with rhyming words and put them on the trucks.

Lesson 55 (crayon/s)

- Students will: identify and write rhyming words
- Brainstorm together with your child words that rhyme with square.
    - fair, pear, mare, rare, share, etc.
- Lesson 55 worksheet
    - Your child will color in the books with words on them that rhyme with bear.
    - They will also write some words. Encourage them to cover over the top of the page and then try to write the rhyming words.

Alphabetical Order

Lesson 56

- Students will: practice alphabetical order
- Sing the alphabet song together.
- Lesson 56 worksheet
  - They will complete an alphabet dot to dot, connecting the letters in order.

Lesson 57

- Students will: practice writing the alphabet in alphabetical order
- Lesson 57 worksheet
  - They will write out the alphabet in order. Encourage your child to sing the song to help them get it correct. They can write in uppercase or lowercase letters.

Lesson 58 (optional: crayon)

- Students will: practice alphabetical order
- Lesson 58 worksheet
  - They will complete the maze by connecting the letters in order, uppercase and then lowercase.
    - They could just draw a line or they could color in the alphabet blocks.

Lesson 59 (scissors)

- Students will: practice putting words in alphabetical order
- They will be putting words in alphabetical order by comparing the first letter in each word.
  - Here are some examples.
    - **Ball** comes before **couch** because **b** comes before **c**.
    - **Shoe** comes before **turtle** because **s** comes before **t**.
- Lesson 59 worksheet
  - Have your child circle the first letter in each word. That's what they will be comparing.
  - Cut out the word strips. Have your child lay them in order based on the first letter in each word.

Lesson 60 (scissors)

- Students will: practice putting words in alphabetical order
- Lesson 60 worksheet
    - This is just like Lesson 59. They will circle the first letter of each word, cut out the word strips, and put them in alphabetical order by comparing the first letters, which comes first in the alphabet.

Writing Sentences – Capitalization and Punctuation

Lesson 61

- Students will: create a proper sentence
- Ask your child what kind of letter does a sentence start with.
    - a capital letter, a big one
- Ask your child how every sentence has to end.
    - with an ending punctuation mark: period, exclamation point, or question mark
- Lesson 61 worksheet
    - They will write a sentence by copying a part from each box in order.
    - Make sure their sentence starts with a capital letter and finishes with an end mark.

Lesson 62

- Students will: choose correct ending punctuation
- Ask your child when you use a period.
    - when you are just saying a regular sentence
- Ask your child when you use an exclamation point.
    - when you are exclaiming something, shouting it
- Ask your child when you use a question mark.
    - when you are asking a question
- Lesson 62 worksheet
    - They will choose the correct ending punctuation.
    - You can encourage your child to read the sentences out loud to help them know what goes at the end.

Lesson 63

- Students will: write the correct ending punctuation
- Lesson 63 worksheet
    - They will write in the correct punctuation at the end of each sentence.

Lesson 64

- Students will: correct the capitalization and punctuation in sentences
- Lesson 64 worksheet
    - Your child will add missing punctuation but can also cross out what is incorrect and write what's correct (such as a lowercase letter at the beginning of a sentence).

Lesson 65

- Students will: write sentences using a period, exclamation point, and question mark
- Lesson 65 worksheet
    - There are places for three sentences. They are supposed to write one with each punctuation mark.

Lesson 66

- Students will: write a knock knock joke
- If you know some knock knock jokes, tell them.
    - I chose knock knock jokes because they happen to use periods, exclamation points, and question marks, all in one.
    - Identify with your child where each would go.
- Lesson 66 worksheet
    - There's an example on the page.
    - Encourage your child to write any knock knock joke. It's okay if it's not funny or doesn't really make any sense! It's a punctuation exercise at its heart.

Lesson 67

- Students will: use each ending punctuation in creating a descriptive animal guessing game
- Lesson 67 worksheet
    - There's an example on the page. They will choose an animal and draw a picture of it.
    - Then they will use a period and exclamation point to write two sentences to describe their animal.
    - They will then write the question, "Who am I?"
        - Your child can surprise you, or if you already have been told what animal it is, you could show it to someone else and have them guess.

Lesson 68

- Students will: write a shape poem
- Lesson 68 worksheet
    - They will identify the shape on the page and write a poem about it in its shape.
    - Encourage them to use a period, question mark, and exclamation point!

Lesson 69

- Students will: write a description using a period, exclamation point, and question mark.
- Lesson 69 worksheet
    - There's a funny picture on the page. They can write anything they want to describe him. They can make up things about him, but they should try to write at least three sentences using each of the ending punctuation marks.

Lesson 70

- Students will: read knock knock jokes to an audience
- Lesson 70 worksheet
    - They can read all or several of these knock knock jokes to an audience, which could be just you.
    - Practice one together using your voice to "show" the exclamation points and question marks.

Spelling

Lesson 71

- Students will: identify beginning and ending sounds in words
- Ask your child what the first letter is in the word gift.
    - g
- Now ask your child what the last letter is and say the word again.
    - t
- When they write words, they will use the sounds they hear in a word and put them together as best they can.
- Lesson 71 worksheet
    - Your child will choose which letter completes the word shown by the picture.

Lesson 72 (scissors)

- Students will: identify the same vowel sound in words
- You'll need to cut out the squares on the page. You'll place them facedown and play a memory/concentration game with the pictures.
    - They will match the vowel sounds, but the words may not look alike.
- To practice you could have them identify the vowel sound in these words: cry, food, free, throw.
    - I, oo/U, E, O
- Lesson 72 worksheet
    - Encourage them to read the words out loud to listen for the similar vowel sounds. They aren't listening for rhymes, but for the same vowel sound.

Writing

Lesson 73 (They will be drawing, so you might want crayons or colored pencils.)

- Students will: make a cartoon
- Lesson 73 worksheet
    - For three days they will be working on a cartoon. There are two boxes on each page. They can draw their character and what happens to the character.
    - Then they write to describe their character and what happened to him.

Lesson 74 (They will be drawing, so you might want crayons or color pencils.)

- Students will: make a cartoon
- Lesson 74 worksheet
    - For two more days they will be working on a cartoon. There are two boxes on each page. They can make a new cartoon if they want or draw what happens to the character next and then write about it.

Lesson 75 (They will be drawing, so you might want crayons or color pencils.)

- Students will: make a cartoon
- Lesson 75 worksheet
    - Today's the last day to be working on a cartoon. There are two boxes on each page. They can make a new cartoon if they want or draw what happens to the character next and then write about it.

Lesson 76

- Students will: choose which descriptive word to use and then describe
- Lesson 76 worksheet
    - They will fill in the blanks with the words from the word box and then write their own sentence.

Lesson 77

- Students will: brainstorm descriptions of a room
- Lesson 77 worksheet
    - They will choose a favorite room and fill in descriptions in each box.

Lesson 78

- Students will: write a description of their favorite room
- Lesson 78 worksheet
    - They will write a sentence using each of the first three description ideas they came up with in Lesson 77.

Lesson 79

- Students will: write a description of their favorite room
- Lesson 79 worksheet
    - They will write a sentence using each of the second three description ideas they came up with in Lesson 77.

Lesson 80

- Students will: draw a picture of their favorite room
- Have your child read over what they wrote in Lessons 78 and 79 and change anything that makes them stumble. You could help with that.
- Lesson 80 worksheet
    - They can draw a picture of the room they've been describing. Then they should present their description to an audience.

Lesson 81

- Students will: write a story
- Lesson 81 worksheet
    - There's a picture on the page of a boat on top of a tree. Ask your child how it got there. Encourage them to be as silly as they want.
    - If the physical writing is hard for your child, you could write for them as they dictate the story. Otherwise, encourage them to try and just spell words however they sound and not worry about getting them all right.

Lesson 82

- Students will: describe their family
- Lesson 82 worksheet
    - This is just a page with lines for writing. They will write about their family. Encourage them to describe the people in their family and not just say their names.
    - If the physical writing is hard for your child, you could write for them as they dictate the story. Otherwise, encourage them to try and just spell words however they sound and not worry about getting them all right.

Lesson 83

- Students will: describe their favorite thing to do
- Lesson 83 worksheet
    - Encourage them to not just tell what it is they like to do but why they like it so much.
    - If the physical writing is hard for your child, you could write for them as they dictate the story. Otherwise, encourage them to try and just spell words however they sound and not worry about getting them all right.

Lesson 84

- Students will: describe what they had for dinner the day before
- Lesson 84 worksheet
    - Encourage them to include what it looked and smelled like
    - If the physical writing is hard for your child, you could write for them as they dictate the story. Otherwise, encourage them to try and just spell words however they sound and not worry about getting them all right.

Lesson 85

- Students will: write a story
- Lesson 85 worksheet
    - Encourage them to be as silly as they want.
    - If the physical writing is hard for your child, you could write for them as they dictate the story. Otherwise, encourage them to try and just spell words however they sound and not worry about getting them all right.

Lesson 86

- Students will: write with an alliteration
- Introduce alliteration to your child.
    - Say the tongue twister: Peter Piper picked a peck of pickled peppers.
    - Ask them what sound they heard in there over and over again.

- All of the main words start with the sound P. That's called alliteration.
- Some other examples are Mickey Mouse, Donald Duck, Peter Pan, worry wart, bumble bee, etc.
- Together you could think of some more alliteration pairs.
- Have them go to their worksheet and copy the sentence and look for an alliteration where at least two words are next to each other that begin with the same sound.

- Lesson 86 worksheet
  - They will copy the sentence on the page.
  - Then they will come up with two words that are an alliteration and use them in a sentence.

Lesson 87

- Students will: learn how a specific verb can make a sentence more exciting.
- Lesson 87 worksheet
  - They will copy the sentence and then try to imitate it in writing their own sentence.
  - Point out to your child how swooping makes it more exciting because it gives a specific action picture of what he's doing. You can brainstorm ideas of some exciting verbs they could use in their sentence.

Lesson 88

- Students will: identify correctly written sentences
- Lesson 88 worksheet
  - Oversee your child doing the first one. They can circle the letter of the correct answer. Go over what makes it the correct answer.
    - It starts with a capital letter, and it ends with correct punctuation.

Lesson 89

- Students will: identify onomatopoeia and use it in a sentence
- Brainstorm with your child words that make the sound they name. The examples on their worksheet for today are tap, buzz, pop, swish. Can you say all of those and make them sound like what they are saying? Can you think of more? These are words you would say in a fun way if you were reading to children.
  - burp, drizzle, splat, bam, boom, hush, achoo, crash, plink, etc.
  - There are lots of them. You can easily come up with more by listing animal sounds: moo, oink, baa, etc.
- Lesson 89 worksheet
  - They will copy the sentence there and then write their own sentence with a sound word.
  - This would be a good one to read aloud or to have your child read aloud.

Lesson 90

- Students will: write a sentence using onomatopoeia
- Lesson 90 worksheet
    - They will read the sound words out loud, saying it like the sound.
    - Then they can write their own sentence. If your child can't think of a word, read through the examples from Lesson 89.

Lesson 91

- Students will: learn about setting
- Introduce the term setting.
    - Have your child think about a book they are reading for school or a favorite book or story they know.
    - Ask your child where it takes place. Can they picture it? What country does it take place in? State? City? Does it mostly take place in a house or in a park, etc.
    - Setting is also when a story takes place. Ask your child when the story takes place. Is it modern day or long ago?
- Lesson 91 worksheet
    - They will draw a picture of the setting of the story.

Lesson 92

- Students will: use the five senses to describe the setting
- Lesson 92 worksheet
    - Have your child use the setting from the day before and write in words to describe what they imagine it looks like, smells like, etc.

Lesson 93

- Students will: write a description of the setting
- Lesson 93 worksheet
    - Your child will take the words from the boxes from the day before and describe the setting.
    - Tell your child that they need to describe the setting so that someone else would picture it just like they do. (They don't have to feel like they need to fill the page.)
    - As always, if the physical part of writing is hard, you can write as your child dictates.

Lesson 94

- Students will: read their description
- Lesson 94 worksheet
    - They will read their description to someone and have them draw the setting they are hearing described.
    - You've already seen their drawing, so it's up to you if you want to do this or have someone else do it.
    - In Lesson 95 they will be revising their description to add in what's needed to improve on what was lacking in this picture.

Lesson 95

- Students will: revise their description
- Look over the pictures in Lesson 91 and Lesson 94. What's different? What's missing from Lesson 94? What descriptions need to be added to get the reader or listener to picture it right?
- Lesson 95 worksheet
    - They can rewrite their description here and add those missing details.

Lesson 96

- Students will: learn the difference between fact and opinion
- Teach your child the difference between a fact and an opinion.
    - A fact is something we know is true. We can see it, feel it, taste it, etc.
    - An opinion is just what someone thinks. Many people may share the same opinion, but it's still just what they think. Others may have the opposite opinion.
    - Brainstorm some examples of facts and opinions. (The first sentences are facts and they are each followed by an opinion.)
        - This is a table. It's nice.
        - You are a girl/boy. You are super special.
        - It's sunny/rainy. It's great/bad weather.
- Lesson 96 worksheet
    - They will decide if each sentence is a fact or an opinion. Remind them that just because they agree with the opinion doesn't make it fact. If it's just what someone thinks about it, then it's an opinion.

Spelling and Grammar

Lesson 97

- • Students will: choose the letters that complete the word
- • Lesson 97 worksheet
    - o They will write in the letters needed to complete each word. Encourage them to try the different sounds out loud in the words to see if they make sense.
    - o There is also a sentence to copy.

Lesson 98

- • Students will: spell words on their own
- • Lesson 98 worksheet
    - o Your child will try to write each word on their own. Say each word to your child and have them write what they hear. Encourage them to read what they wrote to see if it looks right.
        - ▪ Don't help them to spell it. Let them try on their own. Encourage them to repeat the word out loud to listen for the next sound they need to write.
        - ▪ You could read through the whole list and then let them work on their own if you need to.
    - o Here's the list: socks, bird, train, whale, fox, bike.
    - o There is also a sentence to copy.

Lesson 99

- • Students will: identify vowels needed to complete a word
- • Lesson 99 worksheet
    - o Encourage your child to read the vowel sounds in the word to listen for what makes sense.
    - o There is a sentence to copy as well.

Lesson 100

- • Students will: use given letters to spell words
- • Lesson 100 worksheet
    - o They will unscramble the words. Go through the pictures with your child to make sure they are aiming for the correct word.
        - ▪ If they are stuck, encourage them to cross off letters they have used and say the word out loud to listen for what's needed.
    - o There's a sentence to copy as well.

Lesson 101

- Students will: spell words with no visual cues
- Lesson 101 worksheet
  - Read this list of words to your child one at a time. You may repeat it if they want you to, and you could really give them a sentence to help them understand what you are saying, but encourage them to just try their best and don't give them any letters.
    - The list: make, from, very, any, into, three, just, pray, came, been, after, back, big, little, about, where, when, who, why
  - Encourage your child to read the words to see what looks right.
  - Show your child the correct spelling of any incorrect words. Mark which words were spelled incorrectly on the list above. You can use those words again in Lesson 106.

Lesson 102

- Students will: write in correct ending punctuation, complete words by choosing the missing letter
- Lesson 102 worksheet
  - At the top of the page, they will write in the missing punctuation at the end of each sentence. Review with your child if they are stuck. (. ! ?)
  - In the second activity, encourage your child to insert the different letters to see what makes sense and looks right.

Lesson 103

- Students will: choose either the subject or object pronoun to complete a sentence
- Help your child identify when to use the subject pronoun, I, or the object pronoun, me.
  - Ask your child if you should say, "Me likes to play soccer" or "I like to play soccer."
  - Ask your child if you should say, "Give the book to me" or "Give the book to I."
  - That's what they'll be doing on their worksheet today.
- Lesson 103 worksheet
  - You might want to play hangman first, but the top of the page is for them to write in me or I with a capital I. Encourage them to read it in the sentence to hear if it sounds right.
  - Play "hangman" with your child. Really just let them keep guessing until they get it. The word is baked.

Lesson 104

- Students will: practice spelling, use correct capitalization for the word "I"
- Remind your child that the word I, when referring to yourself, is always capitalized no matter where it is in a sentence.
- Lesson 104 worksheet
    - They will write the sentences, correcting the letter I.
    - They will find the words in the word search as well.

Lesson 105

- Students will: identify words that require a capital letter, write spelling words without any visual cues
- Lesson 105 worksheet
    - Read through the directions with your child to review the capitalization rules.
        - Together think of examples of the name of a person (your child's name), place (your state), thing (your street name), day (today's day - like Monday), month (the month you're in).
        - You can help your child through this worksheet if they are missing things.
    - Read your child the list of spelling words. Repeat them and use them in a sentence to help your child understand what word they are writing.
        - fly, green, bang, fine, give, fast, gone, fill, girl, boy
        - Show your child the correct spelling of any words spelled incorrectly. Make a note of which words they are in the list above. You can use these words again on Day 106.

Lesson 106 (scissors)

- Students will: create words out of our sound blends, write spelling words without any visual cues
- Lesson 106 worksheet.
    - Give your child the spelling words for today. Again, don't give your child any of the letters. Encourage your child to say the word slowly and listen for the sounds. You can repeat the words and give sentences.
        - Use any misspelled words from the other days. You can use this list as well to finish the 15 words.
            - lift, tree, red, flag, fell, will, gave, blew, five, log, first, grow, foot, free, for
        - Show your child the correct spelling of any word spelled incorrectly. It's up to you if you want them to practice those.
    - There's a sentence to copy and an activity on the following page.

- Cut out the word parts and let your child make words by pairing up the beginnings and ends of words. There is no final answer. There are many combinations. Your child can make silly words with them too. It's still a practice in blending together sounds to make words.

Lesson 107

- Students will: identify which letter will complete a word
- Lesson 107 worksheet
    - Encourage your child to try all the letters in the blank if they don't know the answer immediately to see what looks and sounds right.
    - There also is a sentence to copy.

Lesson 108

- Students will: practice spelling by completing a word search
- Lesson 108 worksheet
    - Your child will use the list of words to complete the word search.
    - There is a sentence to copy as well.

Lesson 109

- Students will: edit sentences by correcting words that require a capital letter, practice spelling
- Lesson 109 worksheet
    - Your child will identify which words need a capital letter. You can remember together that all names need a capital letter, whether it's the name of a person, place, thing, day, month, etc.
        - You can help your child find any they missed on their own.
    - Play hangman without the hanging man. Just let your child keep guessing until they get it. The word is birthday.

Lesson 110

- Students will: practice spelling, capitalization, writing sentences with quotation marks and exclamation points
- Lesson 110 worksheet
    - Ask your child which words in a sentence need to be capitalized.
        - I, first letter, names
    - Your child will find the words that need to be capitalized.
    - There's a sentence to copy and a spelling list.

- o Give your child the words as usual.
  - ▪ try, moon, barn, grew, going, stop, farther, help, lock, pit, strike, clock, dogs (There are two more blanks.)
  - ▪ Show your child the correct spelling of any incorrectly spelled words.
  - ▪ Have your child write correctly those words on the blanks provided or in other space on the page.

Lesson 111

- Students will: practice the SH blend, be introduced to the concept of nouns
- Introduce the concept of a noun.
  - o A **noun** is a person, place, or thing. Those types of words, words that are people places or things, we call **nouns**. Here are some nouns: girl, downtown, ball. That was a person, a place, and a thing. They are all **nouns**. Susan, Philadelphia and the Pentagon are also a person, a place, and a thing. They are all **nouns**.
  - o Have your child list people, then places, then things, all nouns.
- Lesson 111 worksheet
  - o Your child will identify the nouns on the page.
  - o If your child is unsure in starting, choose a fish and ask if it's a person? a place? a thing? and guide them through thinking about each one until they get the hang of it.
  - o There are words to copy. Ask your child what all the words have in common.
    - ▪ They all begin with SH.
    - ▪ Ask your child what sound the SH makes.
      - • shhhh

Lesson 112
- Students will: practice with the SH blend, be introduced to collective, proper, and common nouns
- Lesson 112 worksheet
  - o Use the worksheet to talk about common, proper, and collective nouns.
    - ▪ Have your child copy the first line of words and together come up with more common nouns. They are nouns with lowercase letters.
    - ▪ Have your child copy the proper nouns. Together come up with other proper nouns, names, nouns that start with a capital letter.
    - ▪ Have your child copy the collective nouns. Nouns that describe a group of things: team, traffic, everyone…
  - o Then your child will write SH into the blanks. Have your child read all of the words out loud as they write.
  - o Make sure they carefully copy the punctuation on the sentence at the bottom of the page.

Lesson 113

- Students will: identify nouns, practice words with the SH blend
- Lesson 113 worksheet
    - They will use the word list to find the words in the word search.
    - They will identify the nouns in the flowers. Check to see if your child remembers what a noun is.
        - a person, place, or thing

Lesson 114

- Students will: identify nouns in a sentence, write words with the SH blend
- Lesson 114 worksheet
    - Show your child how a crossword puzzle works. They are the SH words they have been practicing. Don't spell the words for your child. Let them figure it out themselves.
    - Your child will find the nouns, the people, places, and things in the sentences. There are two in each one.

Lesson 115

- Students will: write spelling words with the SH blend with no visual cues, put words in alphabetical order, identify nouns
- Lesson 115 worksheet
    - Give your child the spelling words. These are words they've been practicing.
        - ship shop shape shine shirt shoe
    - Remind your child of alphabetical order. That's the order of the alphabet like we sing the alphabet song. They will look for words that start with A, then with B, etc. A word that starts with A will come first on the alphabetical order list.
    - When they are finished, they can circle the nouns.

Lesson 116

- Students will: identify nouns, write words beginning with the CH sound
- Walk around your house together finding nouns. Touch the door, "The door is a noun." Everything you can touch is a noun. Find lots and lots of nouns.
- The other activity on their worksheet will be copying words that begin with CH. Have your child read the list of words and identify what sound they all have in common and what letters make that sound.
- Lesson 116 worksheet
    - Your child will draw nouns and then copy words that all start with CH.

Lesson 117

- Students will: identify nouns in a sentence, practice with words beginning with CH
- Ask your child what a noun is.
  - a person, place, or thing
  - That also means it could be the name of a person, place, or thing.
- Lesson 117 worksheet
  - They will underline the nouns in the sentences provided. You can help them after the fact if they have missed any.
  - They just need to add CH to the letters provided to make the words they are practicing this week.

Lesson 118

- Students will: practice spelling words beginning with CH, write rhyming lines
- Lesson 118 worksheet
  - Your child will need to come up with two rhyming words. You can rhyme several words together to get brainstorming if they don't think of something themselves right away.
    - book/hook/look/took
    - bee/three/tree/me/see/free/plea
    - jump/bump/pump/lump/rump/stump
    - etc.
  - Have your child read the rhyme example out loud to hear what it sounds like.
  - Your child will then write two rhyming lines, just short like the example.
  - There is also a word search to practice the CH words.

Lesson 119

- Students will: practice spelling their CH words, identify nouns
- Lesson 119 worksheet
  - Their spelling activity is an unscramble. If they need help, you can remind them that they are their CH words. What do they all begin with?... They can also use the worksheet from Lesson 118 if they are stuck.
  - There is also a sentence to copy. They are supposed to find two nouns in the sentence and write them down.

Lesson 120

- Students will: spell their words without any visual cues, identify nouns
- Lesson 120 worksheet
  - Give your child the spelling words.
    - chin   chip   chop   cheap   church   churn
  - They will find the baskets that contain a noun.

Lesson 121

- Students will: identify nouns within sentences, copy question words
- Lesson 121 worksheet
  - They will find the nouns within each sentence.
    - Every sentence has three.
  - They will copy the question words given for the copywork today. They all begin with WH.

Lesson 122

- Students will: identify proper nouns, practice words beginning with WH
- Remind your child about proper nouns.
  - They are the names of nouns, the names of people, places, and things.
  - Brainstorm some proper nouns: Brian, McDonalds, Pampers…
  - Ask your child what type of letters starts every proper nouns since they are all names.
    - a capital letter
- Lesson 122 worksheet
  - They will identify proper nouns in sentences.
  - They will fill in the missing WH from the question words.

Lesson 123

- Students will: identify proper and common nouns, practice their spelling words using a puzzle
- Ask your child what type of nouns begins with a capital letter because they are names.
  - proper
  - The other type of noun is called a common noun.
- Lesson 123 worksheet
  - There's one each of proper and common noun in the sentence on their worksheet.
  - The sentence is also an example of descriptive writing. They are to come up with ideas for words they could use to describe a meadow.
    - Brainstorm together if they are stuck. There are some examples on the page, but here are some more.
      - rolling, prickly, lively, beautiful, cheery

Lesson 124

- Students will: identify proper and common nouns, practice spelling their question words beginning with WH
- Lesson 124 worksheet
    - They will unscramble their spelling words. If they are stuck, you can remind them that every word begins with WH. They could also refer back to previous pages in their workbook.
    - There is a sentence to copy, and they will find the proper and common nouns in it.
        - Proper nouns begin with a capital letter because they are names.
        - Common nouns are ones that don't begin with a capital letter.

Lesson 125

- Students will: spell words without any visual cues
- Lesson 125 worksheet
    - Give your child the spelling words.
        - who   what   why   where   when   which
    - Then they will write an acrostic poem. That's where each line of the poem begins with a letter from a word.
        - If MOM was your word, the poem could be: Magnificent, Organized, Motherly or Managing the chaos, Opening our home, Multiplying love
    - Maybe your child would like to use their name if it fits (six lines) or the name of a sibling, friend, or pet.

Lesson 126

- Students will: identify proper nouns, practice words with TH
- Ask your child what all names begin with.
    - a capital letter
- Lesson 126 worksheet
    - They will underline the proper nouns.
    - They will copy the new words that begin with TH.

Lesson 127

- Students will: practice their spelling words beginning with TH, brainstorm proper nouns
- Lesson 127 worksheet
    - They just need to fill in TH.
    - They will come up with their own examples of proper nouns. Make sure they are all capitalized.

Lesson 128

- Students will: write proper nouns, practice their spelling words with a puzzle
- Lesson 128 worksheet
    - They have a crossword puzzle to complete.
    - They are to write proper nouns in their lives: family names, where you live, etc.

Lesson 129

- Students will: identify nouns, practice their spelling words beginning with TH
- Lesson 129 worksheet
    - They will unscramble the words from their list this week.
        - If they are stuck, you can remind them that they all begin with TH.
        - They also are on the previous pages.
    - They can then circle the nouns in the words at the bottom of the page and find the proper nouns among them.

Lesson 130

- Students will: write their words without visual cues, identify common and proper nouns
- Lesson 130 worksheet
    - Give your child the spelling list.
        - this that they thing think there
    - There are words for your child to identify as nouns and to classify as either common or proper. And they will write proper nouns as well. Make sure they are starting them with a capital letter.

Lesson 131

- Students will: order words in alphabetical order, identify common and proper nouns
- Check your child's understanding.
    - Ask your child about common and proper nouns.
        - Proper nouns are names of people, places, and things and begin with a capital letter.
        - Common nouns are people, places, and things that aren't names.
    - Ask your child what the order of the alphabet is.
        - ABCD….
        - Ask your child which word comes first in alphabetical order: bear or elephant.
            - bear because B comes before E
- Lesson 131 worksheet
    - They will write the words in alphabetical order.
    - They will identify the common and proper nouns from the words given.

Lesson 132

- Students will: identify synonyms, choose correct pronouns to complete sentences
- Together with your child think of synonyms for these words. (A synonym is a word with a similar meaning.)
    o angry (mad, upset, etc.)
    o small (little, tiny, etc.)
- Lesson 132 worksheet
    o They will choose between the two words written in the train cars to identify the synonym for the word in the train engine.
    o They will then choose the correct pronoun to complete the sentence.
        ▪ Encourage your child to read the sentence out loud with the pronoun they choose to make sure it makes sense.

Lesson 133 (blue and red crayons – or just use other colors)

- Students will: identify nouns and pronouns
- Talk together with your child about pronouns. They replace nouns. We say she instead of Pamela. Ask your child what pronoun they would use to talk about themselves or to talk about yourself.
    o I, you
- Lesson 133 worksheet
    o They will color the nouns: the common nouns blue (or just choose another color) and the pronouns red.

Lesson 134

- Students will: review spelling words
- Lesson 134 worksheet
    o They will use the words on the page to complete the word search and then copy the words.

Lesson 135

- Students will: review
- Lesson 135 worksheet
    o They have questions to answer.
    o If they ask for help, don't give the answer but talk about the topic to remind them (alphabetical order, nouns, etc.)

Plurals and Pronouns

Lesson 136

- Students will: form plural nouns by adding S
- Teach your child the term, plural.
  - Tell your child that the plural of the word is when there is more than one. You have one friend or many friends. Ask the difference between friend and friends.
    - S is added on.
    - In most cases, you add S onto the word to make it plural.
  - Quiz your child with some nouns. Let them form the plural.
    - car/cars (You can lead them by placing it in the sentence I used above. You have one car. You have many…cars.)
    - balloon/balloons
    - cup/cups
    - etc.
- Lesson 136 worksheet
  - They will add S onto the words to make them plural and then they will be copying plural nouns onto the lines provided.

Lesson 137

- Students will: form plurals using S and ES
- The new spelling rule for today is that when a word ends with an X, SS, SH, or CH, then you add ES instead of just S.
- Lesson 137 worksheet
  - They will have to look at each word and see how it ends. If it ends in an X, SS, SH, or CH then they will add ES, otherwise, just S. The list of endings is on their page for them to refer to.
  - They will be copying plural nouns onto the lines provided.

Lesson 138

- Students will: form plurals from nouns ending with Y
- Teach the difference between consonants and vowels.
  - The alphabet is made up of vowels and consonants.
  - The vowels are A E I O U.
  - The consonants are everything else.
- Practice with consonants and vowels.
  - Tell your child different letters and ask if they are consonants or vowels.
    - B, consonant
    - I, vowel
    - L, consonant
    - S, consonant
    - E, vowel

50

- etc.
- Teach your child the rules of making plurals when the words end with Y.
  - When there is a vowel before the Y, they will just add an S to make it plural.
  - Here's the trick though! If there is not a vowel before the Y, if the letter before it is a consonant, then you change the Y to an I and add ES.
- Lesson 138 worksheet
  - You might want to suggest underlining all the vowels where they come before the Y.
    - Those words will just need an S.
  - For the others, they can cross out the Y and write in IES.
  - They will also be copying plural nouns onto the lines provided.

Lesson 139

- Students will: form plurals, identify pronouns
- Introduce pronouns.
  - A pronoun is a word that replaces nouns in a sentence.
  - You could say, "The book belongs to Peter," or you could say, "The book belongs to him." Who's him?
    - Peter
    - The word HIM replaced PETER in the sentence.
  - Try it this way with your child as well. Ask your child to listen for what word we replaced. "The book belongs to Peter," and "It belongs to Peter."
    - The word BOOK was replaced by IT.
  - Try one word. Ask your child what word is used to replace MAYA in the sentence. "Maya called her puppy to come." "She called her puppy to come."
    - SHE replaced MAYA.
- Lesson 139 worksheet
  - You might want to suggest your child start with the bottom of the page since you just talked about pronouns. They are to look for pronouns, words that are used to replace nouns in a sentence.
  - Then they can work on forming plurals. Let them know they can turn back the pages in their workbook to be reminded of the rules.

Lesson 140

- Students will: practice plurals, write a story
- Lesson 140 worksheet
  - They will be writing a story. The goal is to use each type of plural rule in the story. They can use their previous workbook pages for ideas.
  - As always, if the physical part of writing is hard for your child, they can dictate their story to you. Point out the spelling of the plurals, though!

Lesson 141

- Students will: identify correct usage of plurals
- Lesson 141 worksheet
    - If your child can't tell right away which words are correct, suggest they cross ones they know look wrong.
    - You can also remind your child that they can look back at the rules on the previous workbook pages if they aren't sure.
    - There is also a sentence to copy on this page.

Lesson 142 (scissors)

- Students will: learn irregular plurals
- Introduce irregular plurals.
    - Ask your child if there is more than one child do we say, "Childs?"
        - No. Have them tell you the correct way to say it.
    - You can also ask if we say, "Mans," when there is more than one man, and what we say instead.
        - No, we say men.
    - Those are called irregular plurals. They aren't regular. They aren't normal. They don't follow the rules we've learned. They will learn some common ones using the worksheet for today.
- Lesson 142 worksheet
    - Before the sheet is cut up, you might want to have your child do the copywork. Also, have your child read through the page out loud. Each singular word is next to its plural.
    - Then cut out the squares and have your child match them up or play Concentration/Memory to find the matches.
    - You could hold onto these for Lesson 143.

Lesson 143

- Students will: practice irregular plurals
- Today's lesson is just like Lesson 142.
- Lesson 143 worksheet
    - Before the sheet is cut up, you might want to have your child do the copywork. Also, have your child read through the page out loud. Each singular word is next to its plural.
    - Then cut out the squares and have your child match them up or play Concentration/Memory to find the matches.
    - You could add these cards to the ones from Lesson 142 to make the game harder.

Lesson 144

- Students will: review nouns, pronouns, punctuation, capitalization
- Lesson 144 worksheet
    - Go over the directions on the worksheet with your child because there are several sections.
    - You can review for each section.
        - Nouns are people, places, or things.
        - Pronouns are word that replace nouns such as, "Matthew and Mark were two of Jesus' disciples," and "They were two of His disciples."
            - What pronouns were used to replace Matthew and Mark and then Jesus?
                - they, his
        - For punctuation they will just need to add a period, exclamation point, or question mark.
        - For capitalization they are to capitalize the first letter in each sentence and the names of people, places, or things.
    - There is also a sentence to copy.

Lesson 145

- Students will: write words with the a_e spelling pattern
- Write some words for your child such as fame, tale, and made. Have your child read the words and ask your child how they know the A says its name.
    - The silent E makes the A say its name.
- Lesson 145 worksheet
    - All of the words on the page have the same spelling pattern. They are to use the sentences and the pictures for clues as to what word goes in the blank.
    - There is a sentence on the page to copy as well.

Plurals, Pronouns, Writing

Lesson 146

- Students will: learn a new plurals spelling rule (F/V) and practice it
- Introduce the new spelling rule:
    - Ask your child what the plural of leaf is. (one leaf, two…leaves) Ask your child what changed?
        - An S sound was added, but the F sound changed into a V sound.
        - You can do some more if you like. (knife-knives, shelf-shelves)

- o The rule to make these plurals is that you change the F to V. Then the word needs to end in an ES. Sometimes the E is already there. An example: wife becomes wives.
- Lesson 146 worksheet
  - o They will make the plural of each word. They all follow that spelling rule.

Lesson 147

- Students will: practice spelling plurals with a word search
- Lesson 147 worksheet
  - o This is a review of several spelling rules.

Lesson 148

- Students will: practice plural spelling with words ending in Y
- Lesson 148 worksheet
  - o Review the rules for words ending in Y at the top of the page. There is a line for your child to write the vowels as well. Help your child if they aren't sure what the vowels are: A E I O U.
  - o At the bottom of the page they are asked to write a funny sentence using one of the words at the top of the page. If they are stuck, brainstorm together.

Lesson 149

- Students will: practice the formation of sentences with correct structure, identify nouns and proper nouns
- Ask your child to point out a sentence in a book, even just in their language arts book. How do they know it's a sentence?
  - o It starts with a capital letter and ends with a punctuation mark.
- Review nouns and proper nouns with your child. Do they remember what they are?
  - o A noun is a person, place, or thing.
  - o A proper noun is the name of a person, place, or thing and always begins with a capital letter.
- Lesson 149 worksheet
  - o They will rewrite the sentences in the correct order and find the nouns and proper nouns in the words shown at the bottom of the page.

Lesson 150

- Students will: review and practice plural rules, write about a favorite place
- Lesson 150 worksheet
  - o Read through the plurals review on the page. Together you can come up with more examples of each rule.
  - o They can use the examples and rule list to help them write the plurals of the words given on the sheet.

o Then they are to write about their favorite place. They can first copy the sentence starter, but then after adding their favorite place, they should write "because" and tell about what's great about it.

Lesson 151

- Students will: practice plurals and writing creatively
- Lesson 151 worksheet
  - o They just need to choose the correct plural from the options. Encourage them to look at each choice before picking one.
  - o Then they are to write a funny sentence using a plural word. If they are stuck getting started, get them going by giving the sentence starter, "There were two…" Brainstorm what there could be two of. Then brainstorm silly things that could happen to them.

Lesson 152

- Students will: practice the spelling of plurals, identify and write correct pronouns
- Lesson 152 worksheet
  - o Show your child the plural review page (Lesson 150) that they can use to help them write their plurals if needed.
  - o Make sure they understand how to use the crossword puzzle at the bottom of the page.
    - Encourage them to read the sentences out loud with the pronoun in them to listen for if it makes sense.

Lesson 153 (optional: crayon)

- Students will: test their plural spelling skills, identify nouns, proper nouns, pronouns
- Lesson 153 worksheet
  - o The words are on their page for the spelling test this time. They will write the plurals. Tell them not to look back this time, just to try their best.
  - o Then they will follow the directions to identify nouns, proper nouns, and pronouns, the words that replace nouns like I, you, him.
    - They are told to color in the proper nouns. If you don't have anything for coloring, they can shade them or draw a little doodle in them.

Lesson 154

- Students will: identify pronouns
- Practice with some pronouns they haven't seen in their lessons yet.
  - o Touch their book and say, "Give me this." Ask what noun you were replacing by using the word this.

- o Point to their pencil and say, "Give me that." Ask what noun you were replacing by using the word that.
  - o Ask what kind of words are this and that if they replace nouns.
    - ▪ pronouns
- Lesson 154 worksheet
  - o They will "pop" the balloons with pronouns on them.

Lesson 155 (blue and red crayons – or just use any colors)

- Students will: identify pronouns and common nouns
- Lesson 155 worksheet
  - o They just need to follow the directions to identify the nouns and pronouns in the fish.

Lesson 156

- Students will: edit sentences correcting capitalization and punctuation errors
- Lesson 156 worksheet
  - o They will write in capital letters where they belong. They can X out wrong letters and write the capital letter above it.
  - o They will also need to add in ending punctuation.
  - o Use any mistakes to review, but remember to praise everything they got right.

Lesson 157

- Students will: identify correct plural spelling
- Lesson 157 worksheet
  - o They just need to choose the correct plural from the choices given.
  - o Encourage them to look at all the options before choosing one.

Lesson 158

- Students will: write about their day
- Lesson 158 worksheet
  - o They have a blank page for writing. Before they begin, you could talk together about what they did the day before. It doesn't have to be anything special. They can talk about getting up and having breakfast. Can they use sound words, words to describe a smell or taste?
  - o You could take dictation if writing this much would be too hard for your child.

Lesson 159

- Students will: identify the correct pronoun to complete a sentence
- Lesson 159 worksheet
  - They just need to choose the correct pronoun.
  - Encourage your child to read the pronoun in the sentence to make sure it sounds right.

Lesson 160

- Students will: write creatively
- Lesson 160 worksheet
  - They are supposed to choose any book and write what happens next to the main character. If they are stuck getting started, brainstorm different books to choose a character and talk about different ideas about what might happen next.
  - You could write as your child dictates if the physical part of writing is hard for your child.

Lesson 161

- Students will: write correctly formed sentences using proper nouns and pronouns, identify pronouns
- Make sure your child remembers what a pronoun is.
  - It's a word that replaces a noun.
- Lesson 161 worksheet
  - They will follow the directions to write a sentence using a name and then one replacing the name with a pronoun. They can write the same sentence twice if they want and just add the pronoun.
  - Then they will "pop" the pronoun balloons.

Lesson 162

- Students will: choose the correct sentence
- Review proper sentences.
  - Ask your child what a correct sentence begins and ends with.
    - capital letter, punctuation
  - Ask your child what punctuation ends a regular sentence.
    - period
  - Ask your child what punctuation ends a question or excited sentence.
    - question mark, exclamation point
- Lesson 162 worksheet
  - They will choose the correct sentence from the choices given.
  - Encourage them to look at all the options before choosing one.

Review

Lesson 163

- Students will: identify word families
- Lesson 163 worksheet
  - They will put the words into the correct basket that matches their common spelling pattern.
  - There is part of a poem to copy as well. They will be copying it over the coming days.

Lesson 164

- Students will: complete words by filling in their vowel sounds
- Lesson 164 worksheet
  - They will use each vowel sound in one word. They could cross off each one they used already to help them sort through what's available. They could also skip ones they are unsure of and come back to them once they see what hasn't been used.
    - Encourage them to read the word out loud with the vowel sound in it to see if it sounds right.
  - There is part of a poem to copy as well, a continuation from Lesson 163.

Lesson 165

- Students will: complete words using long A spelling patterns, identify pronouns
- Lesson 165 worksheet
  - They will use the word parts in the box to fill in the blanks in the words.
    - Encourage your child to read the sentences out loud to make sure the words make sense.
  - Then they are to go through and look for pronouns in the sentences.
  - There is a poem part to copy as well.

Lesson 166

- Students will: write compound words
- Lesson 166 worksheet
  - They will use the word box to create compound words. Each word part should only be used once.
    - Encourage your child to try the different words out loud to see if they sound right and make sense.
  - There is a poem portion to copy as well.

Lesson 167

- Students will: identify word families
- Lesson 167 worksheet
    - They will put the words into the correct basket that matches their common spelling pattern.
    - There is part of a poem to copy as well.

Lesson 168

- Students will: complete words using long O spelling patterns, identify pronouns
- Lesson 168 worksheet
    - They will use the word parts in the box to fill in the blanks in the words.
        - Encourage your child to read the sentences out loud to make sure the words make sense.
    - There is a poem part to copy as well.

Lesson 169 (scissors)

- Students will: match contractions and their meanings
- Lesson 169 worksheet
    - Have your child read out loud the words and their contractions by reading across the blocks.
    - Then cut out the blocks and have your child match them up, maybe by playing Memory/Concentration, turning over the cards and having them look for matches. You could alternatively hide the cards around the room and they have to find the cards and put the matches together.
    - There is a poem portion to copy as well.

Lesson 170

- Students will: match contractions and their meanings
- Lesson 170 worksheet
    - They will be drawing lines to match the contractions to what words they are replacing.
    - There is a poem portion to copy as well.

Lesson 171

- Students will: order stories and make inferences
- Lesson 171 worksheet
    - Your child will first figure out the order of the story. Have your child read the story in order to make sure it makes sense.
    - Then they will answer the questions making inferences, good guesses.

Lesson 172

- Students will: write plurals
- Lesson 172 worksheet
    - They will write the plurals of the words. They can look back to the plural review page on Lesson 150.

Day 173 (red, blue, green crayons or choose your own colors)

- Students will: identify common nouns, proper nouns, and pronouns
- Lesson 173 worksheet
    - They will color in every flower according to the directions.
    - You can make sure your child knows the terms common nouns, pronouns, and proper nouns. The one we've used the least is common nouns. Those are the lower case nouns, every one that's not a proper noun.

Lesson 174

- Students will: create a character, identify vowel sounds in written and spoken words, write plural words
- Lesson 174 worksheet
    - They are to create a character. On Lesson 175 they will write about their character. They should draw a picture of whomever or whatever it is.
    - The middle section might need your help. They are to match the vowel sounds in the words. You might need to help by sounding out words with exaggerated vowel sounds if they are stuck.
        - You could give an example before you give help.
            - Flop and hot have the same vowel sound even though they don't rhyme.
    - At the bottom of the page they are to write the plural forms of the nouns.

Lesson 175

- Students will: write creatively
- Lesson 175 worksheet
    - This is a page to write a story about their character. If they are stuck to get started, brainstorm together things that could happen to their character.
    - As always, don't let the physical part of writing get in the way of creativity. Go ahead and write the story down as your child dictates if the writing part is hard for them.
    - The point is writing the story, not the writing, so let them spell creatively and don't worry about correcting their spelling on this.

Lesson 176

- Students will: write a comic book
- Lesson 176 worksheet
  - There are five days to work on a comic book story. They can draw pictures and write. A comic is a story without a lot of words.
  - Help your child brainstorm. They could use their character from Lesson 174 if they want.

Lesson 177

- Students will: write a comic book
- Lesson 177 worksheet
  - They have four days to work on this now.

Lesson 178

- Students will: write a comic book
- Lesson 178 worksheet
  - They have three days to work on this now.

Lesson 179

- Students will: write a comic book
- Lesson 179 worksheet
  - They have two days to work on this now.

Lesson 180

- Students will: present a comic book
- Lesson 180 worksheet
  - Today they can finish their story however they like and present their book to an audience.
- Celebrate your child completing first grade language arts!

EP Language Arts 1

Workbook Answers

Lesson 1

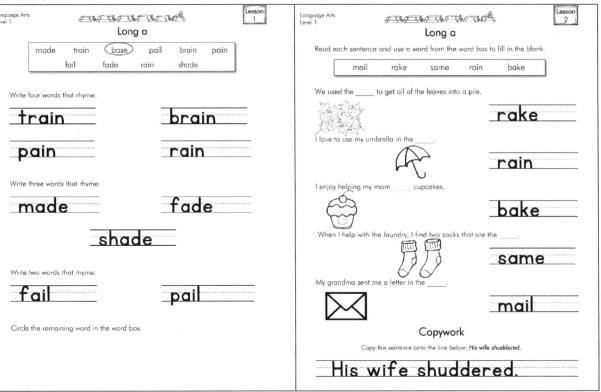

Long a

made	train	base	pail	brain	pain
fail	fade	rain	shade		

Write four words that rhyme:

train   **brain**

pain   **rain**

Write three words that rhyme:

made   **fade**

shade

Write two words that rhyme:

fail   **pail**

Circle the remaining word in the word box.

Lesson 2

Long a

Read each sentence and use a word from the word box to fill in the blank.

mail	rake	same	rain	bake

We used the _____ to get all of the leaves into a pile.

rake

I love to use my umbrella in the _____.

rain

I enjoy helping my mom _____ cupcakes.

bake

When I help with the laundry, I find two socks that are the _____.

same

My grandma sent me a letter in the _____.

mail

Copywork

Copy this sentence onto the line below: *His wife shuddered.*

His wife shuddered.

Lesson 3

Long e

Circle the long e words in the box below. Then find and circle them in the picture.

sun	sea	cloud	pole	reel	boat
	reeds	bird	beak	hat	seat
one	wheel	key	two	man	three

Lesson 4

Long e

First, circle the words below that have the long e sound. Then write them in the blanks under the matching pictures.

tree	snake	bee	horse	leaf	bike
feet	egg	seal	pole	beach	

leaf   **tree**

bee   **beach**

seal   **feet**

Copywork

Copy this sentence onto the line below: *So Jolly Robin thanked him.*

So Jolly Robin thanked him.

64

Lesson 5

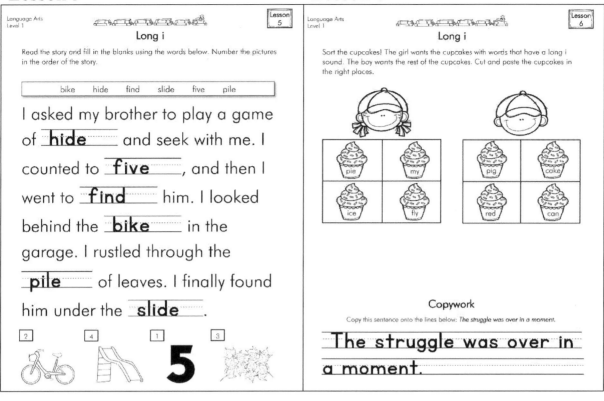

Lesson 6

Lesson 7

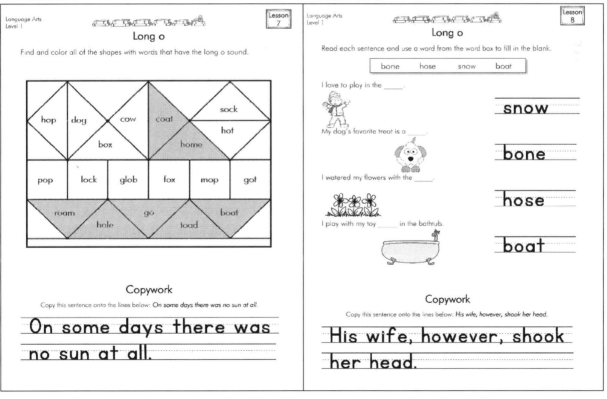

Lesson 8

Lesson 9

Language Arts
Level 1

Lesson 9

Long u

Read the story and fill in the blanks using the words below.

| clue | two | do | blue | you | glue |

I made a card for my sister who turned **two**. I didn't have a **clue** what to make. Then my mom got out the **glue** so I could make a glitter picture. I chose **blue**, her favorite color. I wrote the words, "Happy birthday to **you**." It's fun to see all she is learning to **do**.

Copywork

Copy this sentence onto the lines below: *He had expected to have a ride.*

He had expected to have a ride.

Lesson 10

Language Arts
Level 1

Lesson 10

Long u

Let's make some stew! Color in the vegetables that have words with the long u sound in them.

few *grew* *chew* *true* *blue*

Example: The sky was blue
The clouds were few.

Lesson 12

Language Arts
Level 1

Lesson 12

The Boy Who Cried Wolf

Cut out the following blocks and arrange them in the order they happened in the story.

The boy's father asked him to watch the sheep.

The boy decided the villagers needed to practice a wolf drill.

The father told his son to have no more drills.

The boy thought he saw the shadow of a wolf.

The boy saw a wolf.

No one came to help.

Lesson 13

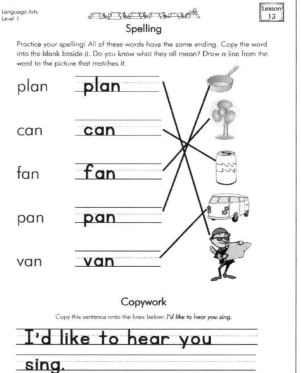

Language Arts
Level 1

Lesson 13

Spelling

Practice your spelling! All of these words have the same ending. Copy the word into the blank beside it. Do you know what they all mean? Draw a line from the word to the picture that matches it.

plan — **plan**

can — **can**

fan — **fan**

pan — **pan**

van — **van**

Copywork

Copy this sentence onto the lines below: *I'd like to hear you sing.*

I'd like to hear you sing.

66

Lesson 14

Spelling Word Search

Find and circle all of your spelling words from Lesson 13. Use the pictures to remind you of the words.

```
F  A  N  B  U  A  N  T  L
A  C  N  Q  D  P  A  E  S
M  R  G  A  N  L  V  A  N
U  O  H  B  C  A  P  W  A
B  E  P  D  A  N  X  Z  T
P  L  A  T  N  L  O  I  S
C  E  N  Y  U  A  F  H  A
```

Copywork

Copy this sentence onto the lines below: *And so all the weeping he might do would be merely wasted.*

And so all the weeping he might do would be merely wasted.

Lesson 15

Goldilocks and the Three Bears

Cut out the following blocks and arrange them in the order they happened in the story.

Goldilocks followed the bird into the forest.	Goldilocks tasted cobbler that was too hot.
The chair broke to pieces.	Goldilocks fell asleep.
The three bears came home.	Goldilocks screamed and ran out of the house.

Copywork

Copy this sentence onto the lines below: *His cousin shook his head at that.*

His cousin shook his head at that.

Lesson 16

Mystery S Picture

Color the words that end in an "s" sound blue. Color the words that end in a "z" sound green.

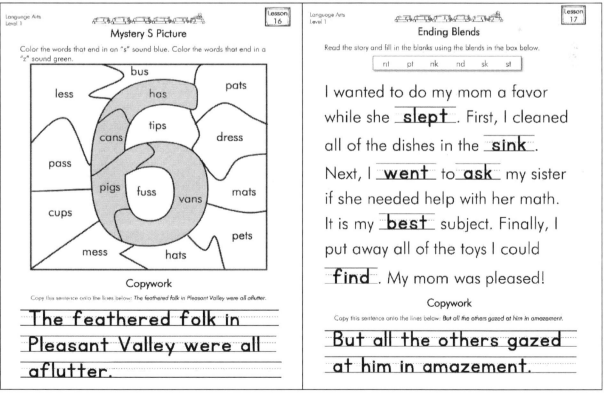

bus
less
pats
has
tips
cans
dress
pass
pigs
fuss
vans
mats
cups
mess
hats
pets

Copywork

Copy this sentence onto the lines below: *The feathered folk in Pleasant Valley were all aflutter.*

The feathered folk in Pleasant Valley were all aflutter.

Lesson 17

Ending Blends

Read the story and fill in the blanks using the blends in the box below.

nt	pt	nk	nd	sk	st

I wanted to do my mom a favor while she **slept**. First, I cleaned all of the dishes in the **sink**. Next, I **went** to **ask** my sister if she needed help with her math. It is my **best** subject. Finally, I put away all of the toys I could **find**. My mom was pleased!

Copywork

Copy this sentence onto the lines below: *But all the others gazed at him in amazement.*

But all the others gazed at him in amazement.

Lesson 18

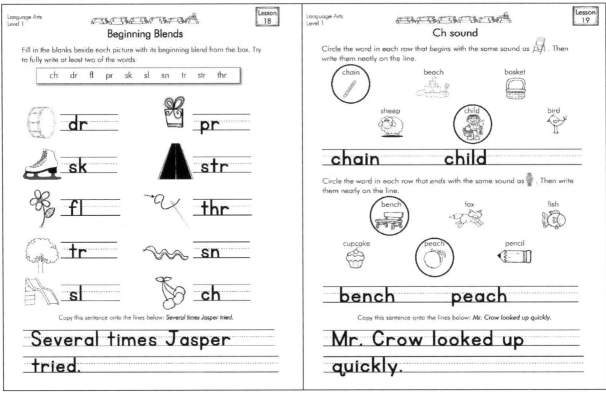

Lesson 19

Lesson 20

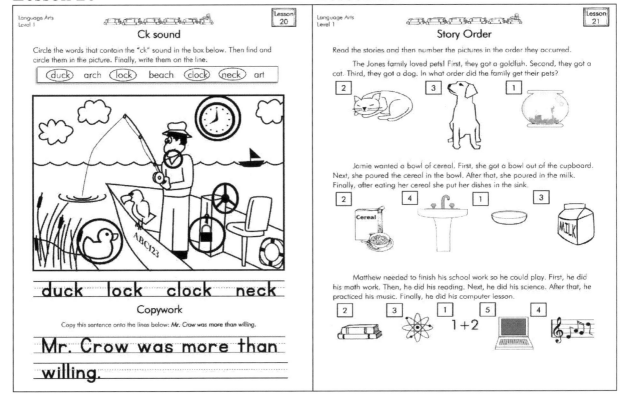

Lesson 21

Lesson 23

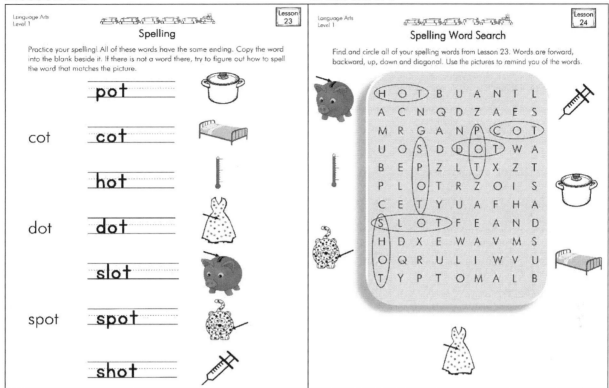

Lesson 23 — Language Arts Level 1

Spelling

Practice your spelling! All of these words have the same ending. Copy the word into the blank beside it. If there is not a word there, try to figure out how to spell the word that matches the picture.

pot

cot   cot

hot

dot   dot

slot

spot   spot

shot

Lesson 24

Lesson 24 — Language Arts Level 1

Spelling Word Search

Find and circle all of your spelling words from Lesson 23. Words are forward, backward, up, down and diagonal. Use the pictures to remind you of the words.

```
H O T B U A N I L
A C N Q D Z A E S
M R G A N P C O T
U O S D D O T W A
B E P Z L T X Z T
P L O T R Z O I S
C E T Y U A F H A
S L O T F E A N D
H D X E W A V M S
O Q R U L I W V U
T Y P T O M A L B
```

Lesson 25

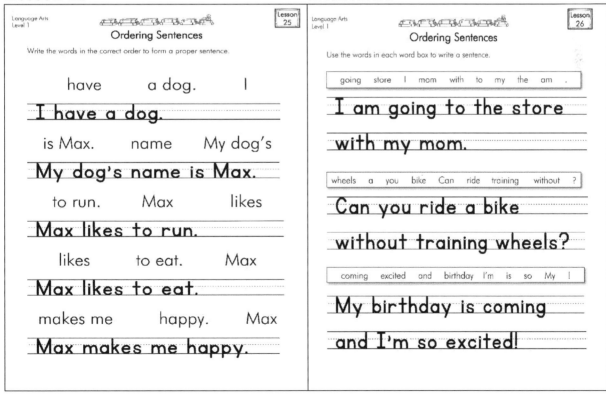

Lesson 25 — Language Arts Level 1

Ordering Sentences

Write the words in the correct order to form a proper sentence.

have   a dog.   I

I have a dog.

is Max.   name   My dog's

My dog's name is Max.

to run.   Max   likes

Max likes to run.

likes   to eat.   Max

Max likes to eat.

makes me   happy.   Max

Max makes me happy.

Lesson 26

Lesson 26 — Language Arts Level 1

Ordering Sentences

Use the words in each word box to write a sentence.

going   store   I   mom   with   to   my   the   am   .

I am going to the store with my mom.

wheels   a   you   bike   Can   ride   training   without   ?

Can you ride a bike without training wheels?

coming   excited   and   birthday   I'm   is   so   My   !

My birthday is coming and I'm so excited!

Lesson 31

Show me the Treasure!

Color brown the words that begin with the same beginning sound in [shovel]. Color yellow the ones that end with the same ending sound in [fish]. Color the rest blue.

Write two words that begin with "sh" and two words that end with "sh" on the line below.

Examples: shoe, shore, ash, dish

Copywork

Copy this sentence onto the lines below: *That was unfortunate for the mice.*

That was unfortunate for the mice.

Lesson 32

Hard and soft th

The girl wants the cupcakes with words that have a hard th like the word *this*. The boy wants the cupcakes with the soft th like the word *thank*. Cut and paste the cupcakes in the right places. Then write 5 "th" words on the lines.

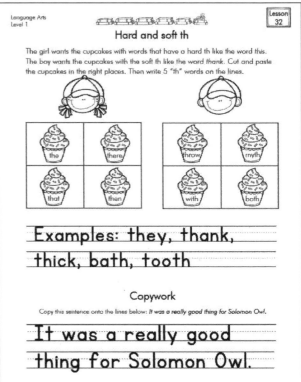

Examples: they, thank, thick, bath, tooth

Copywork

Copy this sentence onto the lines below: *It was a really good thing for Solomon Owl.*

It was a really good thing for Solomon Owl.

Lesson 33

Who Whistled?

Circle the words in the word box that begin with the same sound as [wheel]. Then find those words in the puzzle below. Finally, write them on the lines.

wheel   ship   chop   whale   shape   wheat
plum   whisk   draw   whistle   school   treat

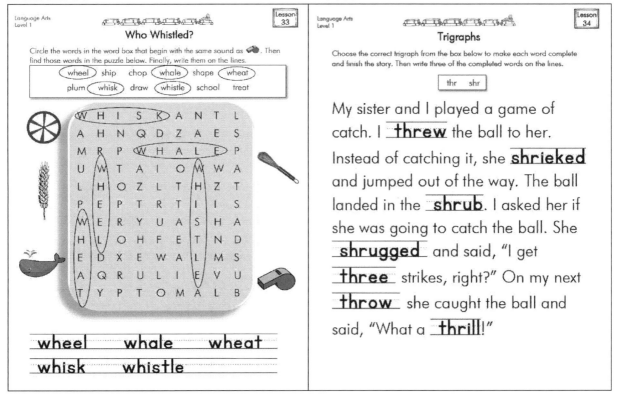

wheel   whale   wheat
whisk   whistle

Lesson 34

Trigraphs

Choose the correct trigraph from the box below to make each word complete and finish the story. Then write three of the completed words on the lines.

thr   shr

My sister and I played a game of catch. I **threw** the ball to her. Instead of catching it, she **shrieked** and jumped out of the way. The ball landed in the **shrub**. I asked her if she was going to catch the ball. She **shrugged** and said, "I get **three** strikes, right?" On my next **throw** she caught the ball and said, "What a **thrill**!"

70

Lesson 35

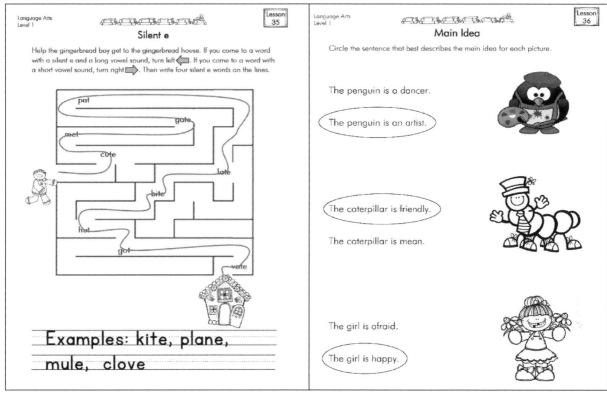

Silent e

Help the gingerbread boy get to the gingerbread house. If you come to a word with a silent e and a long vowel sound, turn left ⬅. If you come to a word with a short vowel sound, turn right ➡. Then write four silent e words on the lines.

pat
gate
met
cute
late
bite
hut
got
vote

Examples: kite, plane, mule, clove

Lesson 36

Main Idea

Circle the sentence that best describes the main idea for each picture.

The penguin is a dancer.

(The penguin is an artist.)

(The caterpillar is friendly.)

The caterpillar is mean.

The girl is afraid.

(The girl is happy.)

Lesson 37

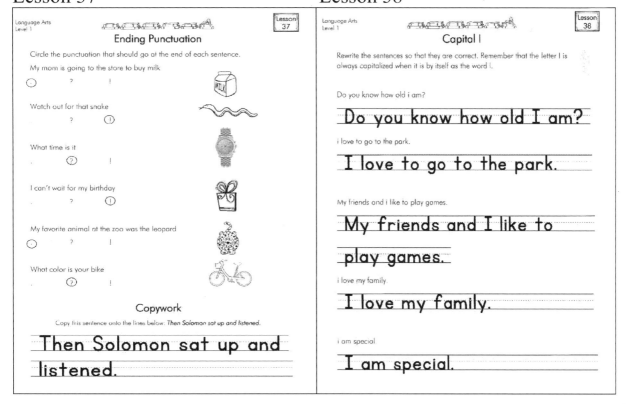

Ending Punctuation

Circle the punctuation that should go at the end of each sentence.

My mom is going to the store to buy milk
(.)   ?   !

Watch out for that snake
.   ?   (!)

What time is it
.   (?)   !

I can't wait for my birthday
.   ?   (!)

My favorite animal at the zoo was the leopard
(.)   ?   !

What color is your bike
.   (?)   !

Copywork

Copy this sentence onto the lines below: Then Solomon sat up and listened.

Then Solomon sat up and listened.

Lesson 38

Capital I

Rewrite the sentences so that they are correct. Remember that the letter I is always capitalized when it is by itself as the word i.

Do you know how old i am?

Do you know how old I am?

i love to go to the park.

I love to go to the park.

My friends and i like to play games.

My friends and I like to play games.

i love my family.

I love my family.

i am special.

I am special.

Lesson 39

Is or Are

Fill in the blanks with either **is** or **are**. Read the sentence out loud to figure out which word fits best.

Today __is__ my sister's birthday.

We __are__ going to the park.

The park __is__ her favorite place.

We __are__ having ice cream.

Her favorite flavor __is__ mint.

My favorite __is__ chocolate chip.

We __are__ going to have fun!

Lesson 40

Is or Are

Fill in the blanks with either **is** or **are**. Use is if the sentence is about one thing. Use are if the sentence is about more than one thing.

The traffic __is__ heavy today.

The cars __are__ moving slowly.

A bus __is__ at the front.

It __is__ stopping.

People __are__ getting on the bus.

The vehicles __are__ moving again.

Copywork

Copy this sentence onto the lines below: *"What have you been eating?" she inquired.*

"What have you been eating?" she inquired.

Lesson 41

Long and Short a

Color in the spaces with words with a short a sound blue. Color in the spaces with words with a long a sound gray. What long a sound picture do you see?

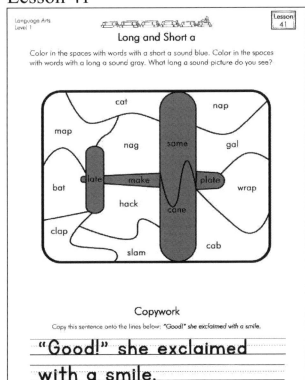

Copywork

Copy this sentence onto the lines below: *"Good!" she exclaimed with a smile.*

"Good!" she exclaimed with a smile.

Lesson 42

Long and Short e

Put all the words with the short e sound in the box with the dress. Put all of the words with the long e sound in the box with the feet.

get	meal	seat	mess	sell
team	ten	bead	seek	gel

get
mess
sell
ten
gel

meal
seat
team
bead
seek

Copywork

Copy this sentence onto the lines below: *It was different with Benjamin Bat.*

It was different with Benjamin Bat.

Lesson 43

Long and Short i

For each sentence, choose the word that best fits and write it on the line.

My dog **bit** his toy.   bit   bite

The gum cost a **dime**.   dim   dime

I love to **slide**.   slid   slide

We have a **pine** tree.   pin   pine

A bird is on the **limb**.   limb   lime

We already **lit** a match.   lit   lite

I **like** the color blue.   lick   like

Lesson 44

Long and Short o

Sort the cupcakes! The girl wants the cupcakes with words that have a short o sound. The boy wants the cupcakes with the long o sound. Cut and paste the cupcakes.

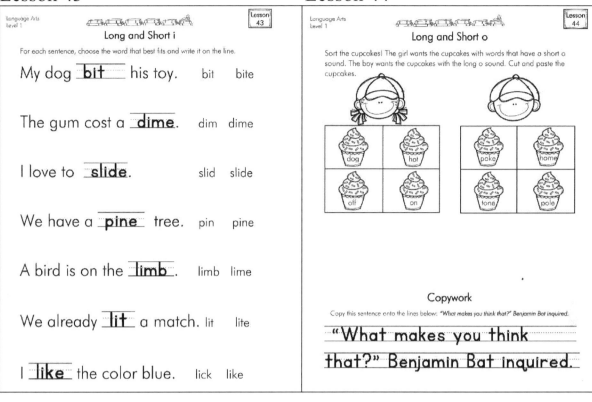

Copywork

Copy this sentence onto the lines below: "What makes you think that?" Benjamin Bat inquired.

"What makes you think that?" Benjamin Bat inquired.

Lesson 45

Long and Short u

Put all the words with the short u sound in the box with the hut. Put all of the words with the long u sound in the box with the cube.

mutt   pup   chute   rug   tube
cute   prune   hug   duke   cup

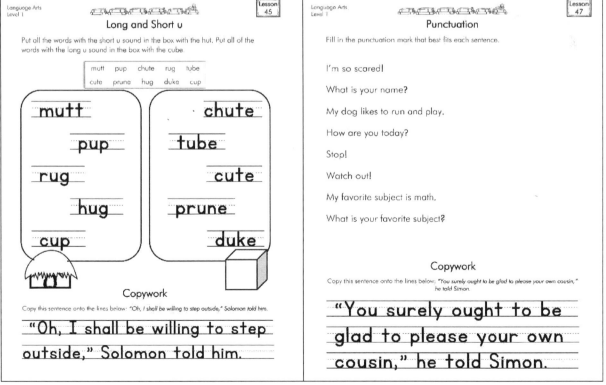

mutt   chute
pup   tube
rug   cute
hug   prune
cup   duke

Copywork

Copy this sentence onto the lines below: "Oh, I shall be willing to step outside," Solomon told him.

"Oh, I shall be willing to step outside," Solomon told him.

Lesson 47

Punctuation

Fill in the punctuation mark that best fits each sentence.

I'm so scared!

What is your name?

My dog likes to run and play.

How are you today?

Stop!

Watch out!

My favorite subject is math.

What is your favorite subject?

Copywork

Copy this sentence onto the lines below: "You surely ought to be glad to please your own cousin," he told Simon.

"You surely ought to be glad to please your own cousin," he told Simon.

Lesson 49

Picture Order

Put these pictures in the order they would happen. Write the number order in the boxes beside the pictures.

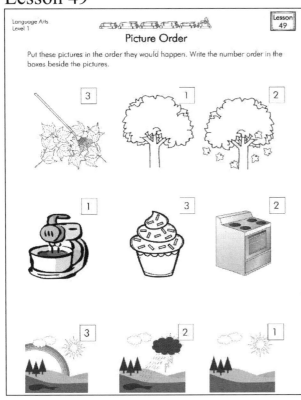

Lesson 51

Ar Blend

These "ar" words are scrambled! Unscramble them and then find them in the puzzle below. Use the pictures for hints if you need them.

bark	car	shark	cart	dart	chart

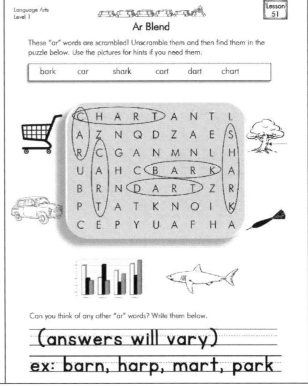

Can you think of any other "ar" words? Write them below.

(answers will vary)

ex: barn, harp, mart, park

Lesson 52

Blends: ir, ur, er

Fill in the blank with the proper blend from the box.

ir	ur	er

I like **turkey** and gravy.

I got **third** place in the race.

Do you like beef **jerky**?

Dancers like to spin and **twirl**.

The farmer **churned** the butter.

Lesson 53

Or sound

Circle the words that contain the "or" sound in the box below. Then find and circle them in the picture.

(fork)	barn	curl	(shorts)	(horn)	(storm)	art

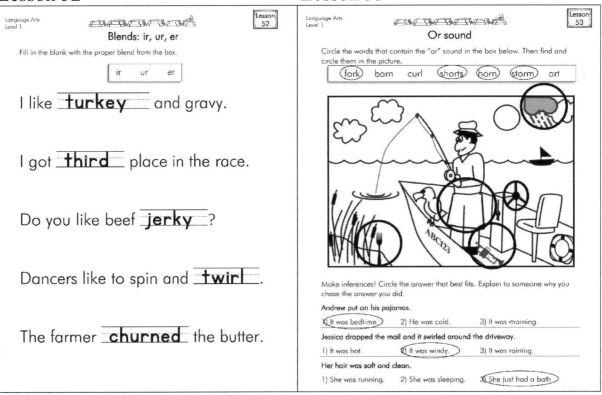

Make inferences! Circle the answer that best fits. Explain to someone why you chose the answer you did.

Andrew put on his pajamas.

1) It was bedtime.   2) He was cold.   3) It was morning.

Jessica dropped the mail and it swirled around the driveway.

1) It was hot.   2) It was windy.   3) It was raining.

Her hair was soft and clean.

1) She was running.   2) She was sleeping.   3) She just had a bath.

74

Lesson 54

Where's My Tire?

The trucks are missing their tires! Cut and paste the tires with words that rhyme with "tire" onto the trucks. Then write "fire" and 3 words that rhyme with it.

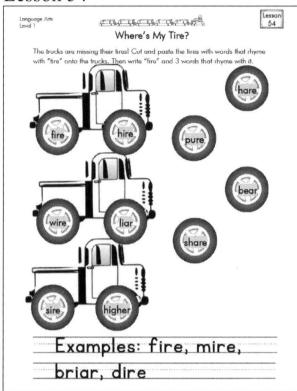

Examples: fire, mire, briar, dire

Lesson 55

Reader Bear

Mr. Bear only wants to read books with words that rhyme with his name. Color in the books that rhyme with "bear." Then write five words that rhyme with bear. Can you think of any new ones?

Examples: mare, flair, hare, bare, tear

Lesson 56

A-B-C

Do you remember your ABCs? Connect the dots in alphabetical order to reveal the picture.

What "ck" word did you draw?

duck

Lesson 58

A-B-C

Get the bookworm to the rest of the books! Start with the capital A in the top row and then move to the B and on through the alphabet in order. Once you get to Z, move to the lowercase a and keep continuing through the alphabet until you find the books.

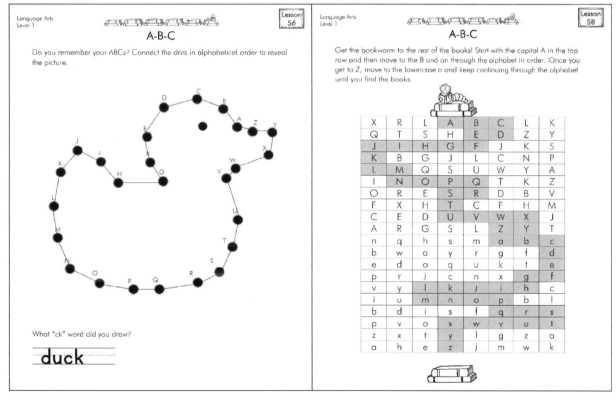

X	R	L	A	B	C	L	K
Q	T	S	H	E	D	Z	Y
J	I	H	G	F	J	K	S
K	B	G	J	L	C	N	P
L	M	Q	S	U	W	Y	A
I	N	O	P	Q	T	K	Z
O	R	E	S	R	D	B	V
F	X	H	T	C	F	H	M
C	E	D	U	V	W	X	J
A	R	G	S	L	Z	Y	T
n	q	h	s	m	a	b	c
b	w	a	y	r	g	f	d
e	d	o	q	u	k	t	e
p	r	j	c	n	x	g	f
v	y	l	k	j	i	h	c
i	u	m	n	o	p	b	l
b	d	i	s	f	q	r	s
p	v	o	x	w	v	u	t
z	x	t	y	l	g	z	a
a	h	e	z	j	m	w	k

75

Lesson 59

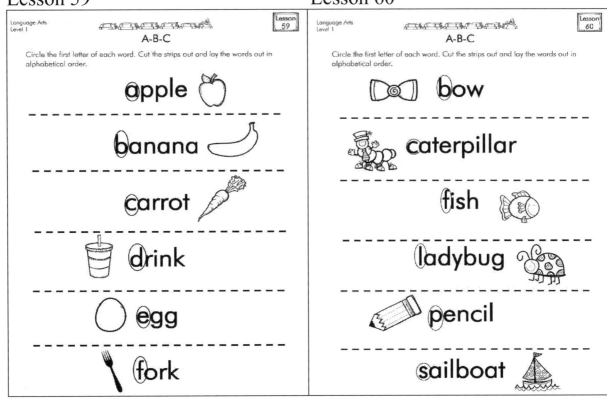

Lesson 60

Lesson 62

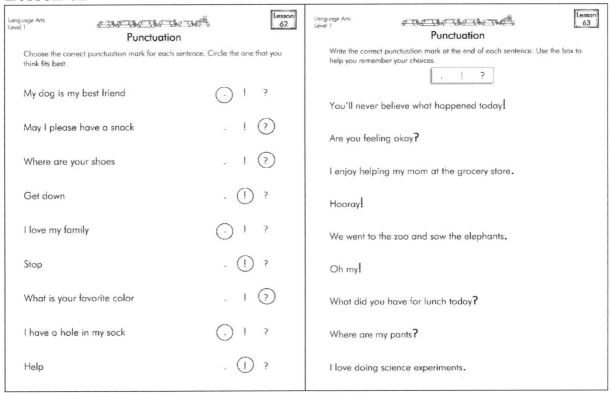

Lesson 63

Lesson 64

Correct the Sentences

Correct the sentences below. Remember that all sentences must begin with a capital letter and end with proper punctuation.

<u>M</u>y favorite animal is a koala bear<u>.</u>

We are going to church in the morning<u>.</u>

<u>H</u>ave you ever traveled out of the country?

<u>W</u>hat are we having for dinner tonight<u>?</u>

<u>I</u>t is so hot outside!

<u>I</u>'m freezing<u>!</u>

What is your name<u>?</u>

I love pizza<u>.</u>

Bonus tricky one:
<u>M</u>y dad's name is Steve<u>.</u>?<u>.</u>

Lesson 71

Phonics Fishing

Help the fisherman catch the fish that properly completes the word. Circle the fish with the right beginning or ending letter.

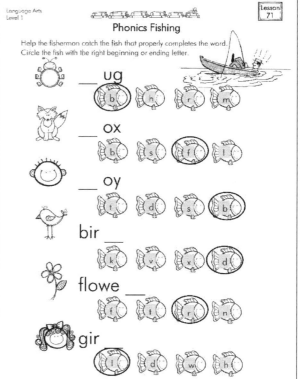

__ ug

__ ox

__ oy

bir __

flowe __

gir __

Lesson 72

Matching

Match the vowel sounds. Cut out the squares, mix them up and lay them face down on the table. Play a game of Memory, matching words that have the same vowel sound (they may be spelled differently).

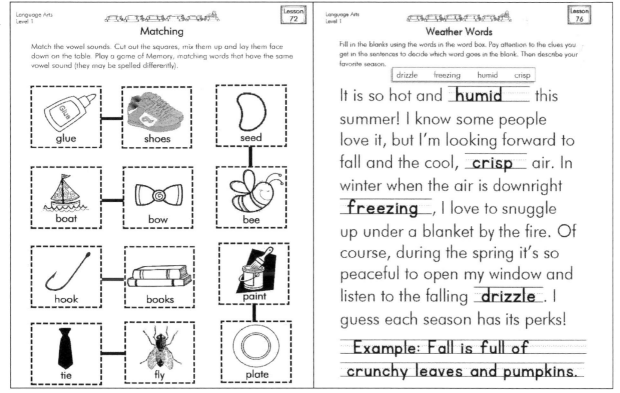

glue — shoes — seed

boat — bow — bee

hook — books — paint

tie — fly — plate

Lesson 76

Weather Words

Fill in the blanks using the words in the word box. Pay attention to the clues you get in the sentences to decide which word goes in the blank. Then describe your favorite season.

| drizzle | freezing | humid | crisp |

It is so hot and **humid** this summer! I know some people love it, but I'm looking forward to fall and the cool, **crisp** air. In winter when the air is downright **freezing**, I love to snuggle up under a blanket by the fire. Of course, during the spring it's so peaceful to open my window and listen to the falling **drizzle**. I guess each season has its perks!

<u>Example: Fall is full of crunchy leaves and pumpkins.</u>

Lesson 88

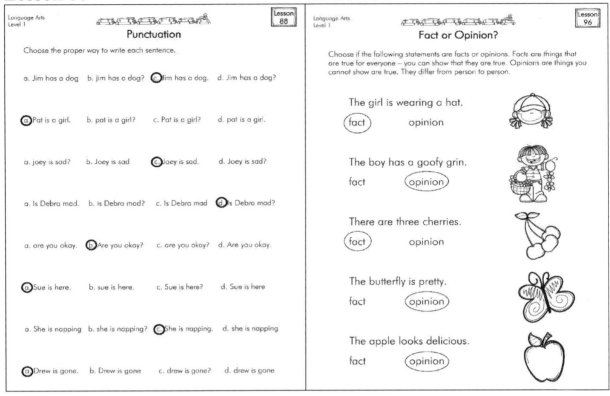

Lesson 96

Lesson 97

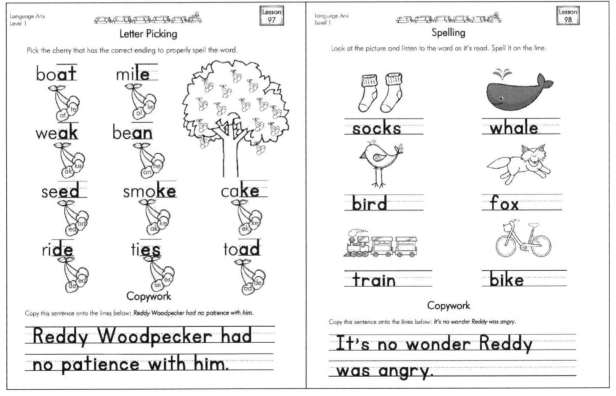

Lesson 98

Lesson 99

Vowel Pairing

Use the apples to pick the vowels that are missing from each word.

squ**i**rrel   b**oa**t

week   babies

suit   plain   spoon

read   toes   oink

Copywork

Copy this sentence onto the lines below: *Then Frisky sat on a limb and glared at him.*

Then Frisky sat on a limb
and glared at him.

Lesson 100

Spelling

Unscramble the letters to spell the words that match the pictures.

d i b r   **bird**

t b a o   **boat**

e f t e   **feet**

a l e s   **seal**

Copywork

Copy this sentence onto the lines below: *Frisky did not intend to go hungry when winter came.*

Frisky did not intend to go
hungry when winter came.

Lesson 102

Punctuation

Fill in the punctuation mark that best fits each sentence.

I'm so excited!

When is your birthday?

My sister loves to sing.

I enjoy dancing.

Help!

What is your favorite food?

How old are you?

Spelling

Fill in the missing letter.

g**i**rl   f**r**om   pr**a**y

i u e o   l r y a   o i a u

h**u**nt   cav**e**   do**w**n

a o u e   u l e r   e z a w

Lesson 103

I or Me

Fill in the blank with I or me to make the sentence correct.

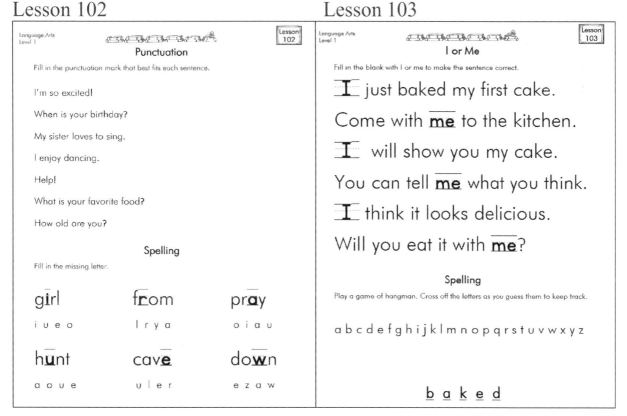

I just baked my first cake.

Come with **me** to the kitchen.

I will show you my cake.

You can tell **me** what you think.

I think it looks delicious.

Will you eat it with **me**?

Spelling

Play a game of hangman. Cross off the letters as you guess them to keep track.

a b c d e f g h i j k l m n o p q r s t u v w x y z

b a k e d

79

Lesson 104

Capital I

Rewrite the sentences so that they are correct. Then practice your spelling by finding the words from the box in the puzzle at the bottom of the page.

i love spaghetti.

I love spaghetti.

Do you think i am smart?

Do you think I am smart?

i always try my best.

I always try my best.

May i go first?

May I go first?

F	A	P	A	R	T	P	T	L
I	C	N	Q	D	Z	I	R	P
L	R	G	I	F	T	N	Y	U
L	W	H	I	P	A	E	P	R
B	I	N	D	E	N	X	Z	X
P	C	A	L	L	T	A	R	S

fill	gift	whip	pine	try	call	trap

Lesson 105

Capitalization

Underline the words in each sentence that need to be capitalized. Remember that all names are capitalized – names of people, places, days, months, etc. Also remember that each sentence should start with a capital letter. Then use the lines at the bottom for your spelling words.

the children were excited for their trip to the zoo on friday.

mr. smith brought the ham for our easter meal.

the fire station is on main street.

mary's favorite holiday is christmas.

in july we see a lot of fireworks.

fly	fast
green	gone
bang	fill
fine	girl
give	boy

Lesson 107

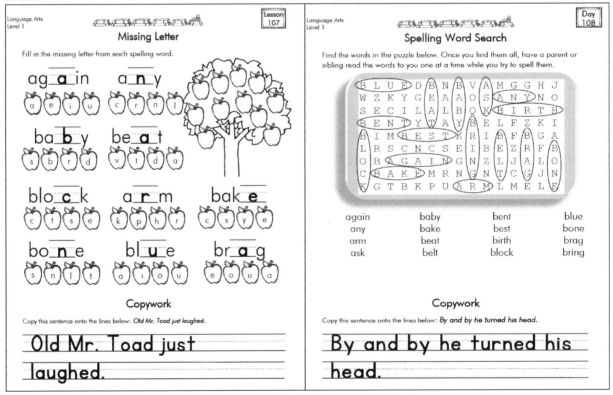

Missing Letter

Fill in the missing letter from each spelling word.

ag **a** in   a e i u

a **n** y   c r n t

ba **b** y   s b r d

be **a** t   v t d a

blo **c** k   c t s e k

a **r** m   k p h r

bak **e**   c s y e

bo **n** e   s n l t

blu **e**   a i o u

br **a** g   e o u a

Copywork

Copy this sentence onto the lines below: *Old Mr. Toad just laughed.*

Old Mr. Toad just laughed.

Lesson 108

Spelling Word Search

Find the words in the puzzle below. Once you find them all, have a parent or sibling read the words to you one at a time while you try to spell them.

B	L	U	E	D	B	N	B	V	A	M	G	G	H	J
W	Z	K	Y	G	E	A	A	O	S	A	N	Y	N	O
S	E	C	I	L	A	L	B	O	K	B	I	R	T	H
B	E	N	T	Y	T	A	Y	B	E	L	F	Z	K	I
B	I	M	B	E	S	T	K	R	I	E	F	B	G	A
L	R	S	C	N	C	S	E	I	B	E	Z	R	F	B
O	B	A	G	A	I	N	G	N	Z	L	J	A	L	O
C	B	A	K	E	M	R	N	G	N	T	C	G	J	N
K	G	T	B	K	P	U	A	R	M	L	M	E	L	E

again	baby	bent	blue
any	bake	best	bone
arm	beat	birth	brag
ask	belt	block	bring

Copywork

Copy this sentence onto the lines below: *By and by he turned his head.*

By and by he turned his head.

Lesson 109

Capitalization

Underline the words in each sentence that need to be capitalized. Get a parent to help you if you need to. (All names are capitalized – names of people, places, days, months, etc. Also remember that each sentence should start with a capital letter.)

the campbell kids were playing in their tennessee yard.

mrs. blane went to the grocery store.

i live in the united states of america.

what is your favorite month?

my birthday is on a saturday this year.

Spelling

Play a game of hangman. Cross off the letters as you guess them to keep track.

a b c d e f g h i j k l m n o p q r s t u v w x y z

b i r t h d a y

Lesson 110

Capitalization

Underline the words in each sentence that should be capitalized. Add punctuation to the end of each sentence. Then write your spelling words.

did you see james kick that ball?

mary is screaming for help!

you and i should meet for lunch on friday.

Copywork

Copy this sentence onto the line below: *"Next time I'll get him!"*

"Next time I'll get him!"

Lesson 111

Fishing for Nouns

A **noun** is a person, place or thing. Jeffrey, post office, ball – those are all nouns. Circle the fish below that contain nouns.

food, toy, car, write, eat, cow, desk, chair, dad, loud

Copywork

Copy these words onto the lines below: *ship shop shape shine shirt shoe*

ship   shop   shape
shine   shirt   shoe

Lesson 112

Different Nouns

A **noun** is a person, place or thing. There are different types of nouns. Copy the word into the blanks as you learn about nouns.

Common nouns:

girl   church

girl   **church**

Proper nouns: name a *specific* person, place or thing

Carol   Calvary

Carol   **Calvary**

Collective nouns: name a *group* of people, places or things

family   congregation

family   **congregation**

Fill in the missing "sh" to complete the spelling words below.

shape   shine   ship

shirt   shop

Copy this sentence onto the line below: *"That's good," said she.*

"That's good," said she.

Lesson 113

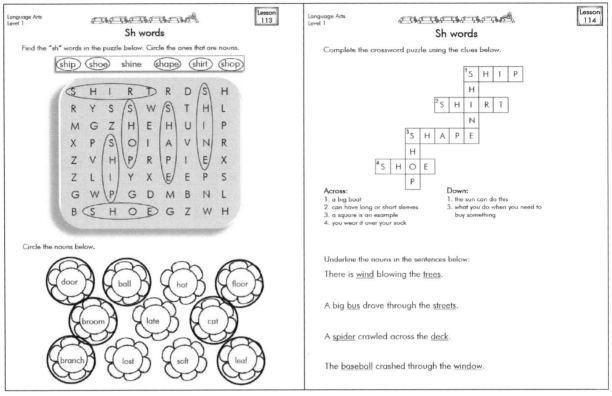

Language Arts
Level 1

Sh words

Find the "sh" words in the puzzle below. Circle the ones that are nouns.

(ship) (shoe) shine (shape) (shirt) (shop)

```
S H I R T R D S H
R Y S S W S T H L
M G Z H E H U I P
X P S O I A V N R
Z V H P R P I E X
Z L I Y X E E P S
G W P G D M B N L
B S H O E G Z W H
```

Circle the nouns below.

door ball hot floor

broom late cat

branch lost soft leaf

Lesson 114

Language Arts
Level 1

Sh words

Complete the crossword puzzle using the clues below.

```
          ¹S H I P
            H
          ²S H I R T
            N
    ³S H A P E
      H
    ⁴S H O E
      P
```

Across:
1. a big boat
2. can have long or short sleeves
3. a square is an example
4. you wear it over your sock

Down:
1. the sun can do this
3. what you do when you need to buy something

Underline the nouns in the sentences below:

There is wind blowing the trees.

A big bus drove through the streets.

A spider crawled across the deck.

The baseball crashed through the window.

Lesson 115

Language Arts
Level 1

Spelling

Write your spelling words as they are read to you. These are the words from your lesson 111 copywork.

ship   shine

shop   shirt

shape   shoe

Alphabetical Order

Put these words in alphabetical order on the lines below. Circle the nouns.

(cage) (tree) (food) eat (milk) drive (bank) pretty (apple) win

1 apple   6 food
2 bank   7 milk
3 cage   8 pretty
4 drive   9 tree
5 eat   10 win

Lesson 117

Language Arts
Level 1

Noun Hunt

Underline all of the nouns in this sentence.

His big eyes filled with tears as he looked at Danny

Meadow Mouse for Danny was all torn and hurt by

the cruel claws of Hooty the Owl, and you know Peter

has a very tender heart.

Fill in the missing ch from the words below.

chin   chip

chop   cheap

church   churn

82

Lesson 118

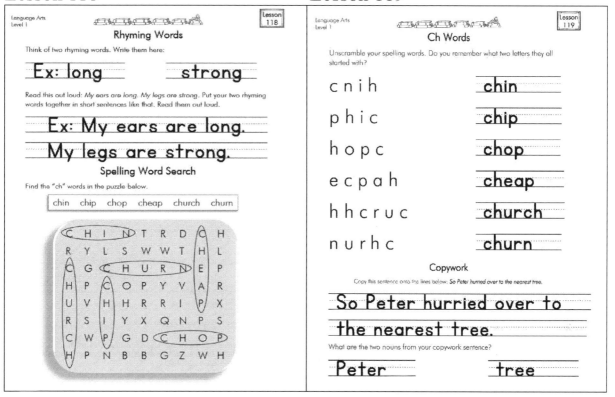

Lesson 119

Language Arts
Level 1

Ch Words

Unscramble your spelling words. Do you remember what two letters they all started with?

c n i h   **chin**

p h i c   **chip**

h o p c   **chop**

e c p a h   **cheap**

h h c r u c   **church**

n u r h c   **churn**

Copywork

Copy this sentence onto the lines below: *So Peter hurried over to the nearest tree.*

So Peter hurried over to the nearest tree.

What are the two nouns from your copywork sentence?

Peter   **tree**

Lesson 120

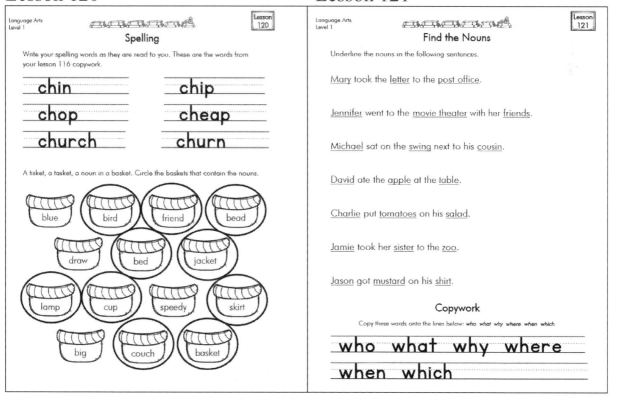

Lesson 121

Language Arts
Level 1

Find the Nouns

Underline the nouns in the following sentences.

<u>Mary</u> took the <u>letter</u> to the <u>post office</u>.

<u>Jennifer</u> went to the <u>movie theater</u> with her <u>friends</u>.

<u>Michael</u> sat on the <u>swing</u> next to his <u>cousin</u>.

<u>David</u> ate the <u>apple</u> at the <u>table</u>.

<u>Charlie</u> put <u>tomatoes</u> on his <u>salad</u>.

<u>Jamie</u> took her <u>sister</u> to the <u>zoo</u>.

<u>Jason</u> got <u>mustard</u> on his <u>shirt</u>.

Copywork

Copy these words onto the lines below: *who what why where when which*

who what why where when which

Lesson 122

Proper Nouns

Proper nouns are names of people, places, or things. Underline the proper nouns in the following sentences.

<u>Mr. Davis</u> went to <u>Pittsburgh</u> last <u>Sunday</u>.

My brother, <u>Stephen</u>, works at <u>McDonald's</u>.

<u>Rachel</u> took a jog in <u>Central Park</u>.

<u>Clara</u> went to school at <u>Lincoln Elementary</u>.

<u>Natalie's</u> birthday is <u>Saturday</u>.

Fill in the missing wh from the words below.

who   **wh**en

what   **wh**ere

why   **wh**ich

Lesson 123

Wh Words

Find the "wh" words in the puzzle below.

who	what	why	when	where	which

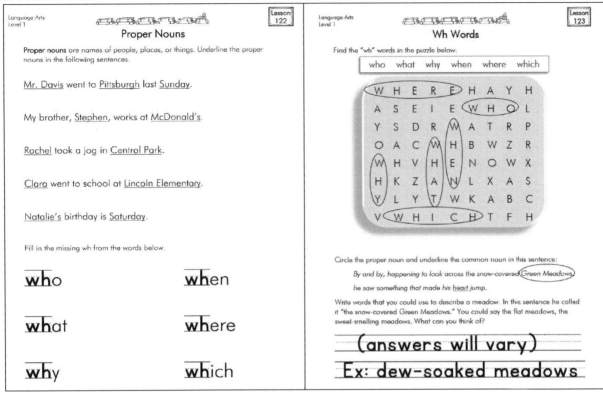

Circle the proper noun and underline the common noun in this sentence:

By and by, happening to look across the snow-covered Green Meadows, he saw something that made his heart jump.

Write words that you could use to describe a meadow. In this sentence he called it "the snow-covered Green Meadows." You could say the flat meadows, the sweet-smelling meadows. What can you think of?

(answers will vary)

Ex: dew-soaked meadows

Lesson 124

Wh Words

Unscramble your spelling words. Do you remember what two letters they all started with?

h w o   **who**

h t a w   **what**

y w h   **why**

e h w n   **when**

r e w e h   **where**

h i w h c   **which**

Copywork

Copy this sentence onto the lines below: *Peter Rabbit sat in his secretest place in the dear Old Briar-patch.*

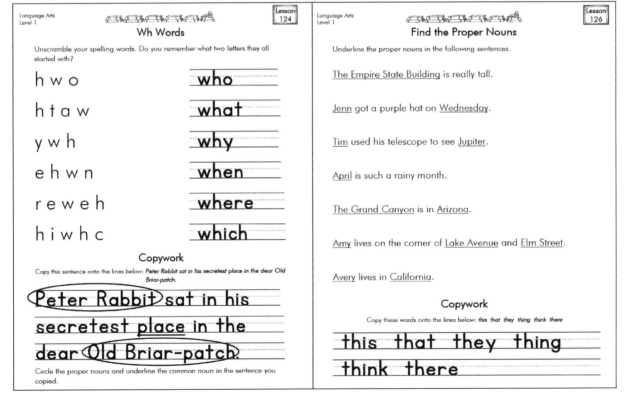

Peter Rabbit sat in his secretest place in the dear Old Briar-patch.

Circle the proper nouns and underline the common noun in the sentence you copied.

Lesson 126

Find the Proper Nouns

Underline the proper nouns in the following sentences.

<u>The Empire State Building</u> is really tall.

<u>Jenn</u> got a purple hat on <u>Wednesday</u>.

<u>Tim</u> used his telescope to see <u>Jupiter</u>.

<u>April</u> is such a rainy month.

<u>The Grand Canyon</u> is in <u>Arizona</u>.

<u>Amy</u> lives on the corner of <u>Lake Avenue</u> and <u>Elm Street</u>.

<u>Avery</u> lives in <u>California</u>.

Copywork

Copy these words onto the lines below: *this that they thing think there*

this that they thing think there

Lesson 127

Th Words

Fill in the missing th from the words below.

this   **th**ing

that   **th**ink

they   **th**ere

Can you think of six proper nouns? Remember to capitalize them!

Lesson 128

Th Words

Find the "th" words in the puzzle below.

| this | that | they | thing | think | there |

```
T H E R E T F Y H
R H G F I H D F T
S K L P J I K R H
Z M Q N H S U Z E
T H A T G Z F W Y
P T H T H I N K S
T H Y R B E L B C
V T H I N G T F H
```

List all the proper nouns you can think of. Some examples are: the names of everyone in your family, the place you live, the name of your church, the name of some local schools.

(answers will vary)
Examples: Liz, Holly,
Alaska, Fox Road, Iowa
Marengo High School

Lesson 129

Th Words

Unscramble your spelling words. Do you remember what two letters they all started with?

s t h i   this
t t a h   that
y t e h   they
g t n i h   thing
k t n i h   think
e t r h e   there

Circle the nouns below. Put a line under the proper nouns below.

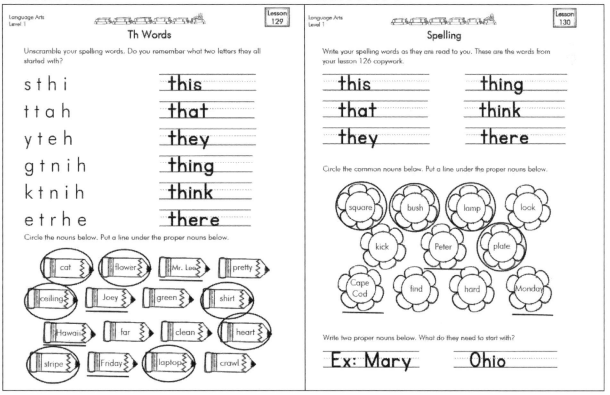

Lesson 130

Spelling

Write your spelling words as they are read to you. These are the words from your lesson 126 copywork.

this   thing
that   think
they   there

Circle the common nouns below. Put a line under the proper nouns below.

square   bush   lamp   look
kick   Peter   plate
Cape Cod   find   hard   Monday

Write two proper nouns below. What do they need to start with?

Ex: Mary   Ohio

85

Lesson 131

Alphabetical Order

Put these words in alphabetical order on the lines below. Circle the nouns.

(bear) jump sweet (film) (zebra) run (yak) (oar) good (police)

1 bear   6 police

2 film   7 run

3 good   8 sweet

4 jump   9 yak

5 oar   10 zebra

Circle the common nouns below. Put a line under the proper nouns below.

mad   cloud   Emily   friend

baby   lips   over

van   France   take   quickly

Lesson 132

Synonyms

Synonyms are words that mean the same thing. *Start* and *begin* are synonyms.
Circle the train car that is a synonym for the train engine.

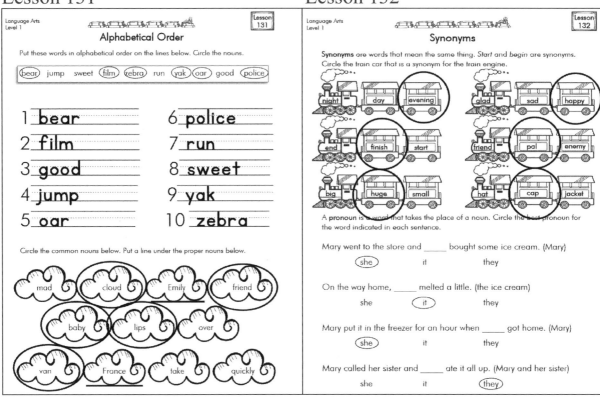

night   day   evening   glad   sad   happy

end   finish   start   friend   pal   enemy

big   huge   small   hat   cap   jacket

A **pronoun** is a word that takes the place of a noun. Circle the best pronoun for the word indicated in each sentence.

Mary went to the store and _____ bought some ice cream. (Mary)
she   it   they

On the way home, _____ melted a little. (the ice cream)
she   it   they

Mary put it in the freezer for an hour when _____ got home. (Mary)
she   it   they

Mary called her sister and _____ ate it all up. (Mary and her sister)
she   it   they

Lesson 133

Fishing for Nouns

Color red the fish below that contain common nouns (circled). Color blue the fish that contain pronouns (squared).

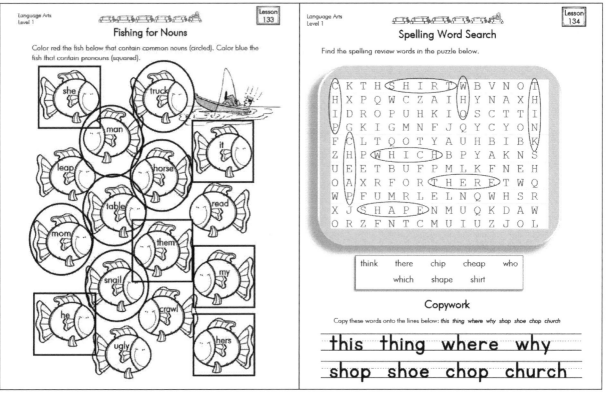

Lesson 134

Spelling Word Search

Find the spelling review words in the puzzle below.

```
C K T H S H I R T W B V N O I
H X P Q W C Z A I H Y N A X H
I D R O P U H K I O S C T T I
P G K I G M N F J Q Y C Y O N
F C L T Q O T Y A U H B I B K
Z H P W H I C H B P Y A K N S
U E E T B U F P M L K F N E H
O A X R F O R T H E R E T W Q
W P F U M R L E L N Q W H S R
X J S H A P E N M U Q K D A W
O R Z F N T C M U I U Z J O L
```

think	there	chip	cheap	who
which	shape	shirt		

Copywork

Copy these words onto the lines below: *this thing where why shop shoe chop church*

this thing where why
shop shoe chop church

Lesson 135

Grammar Review

Answer the questions below by filling in the square beside your choice.

Which of these words comes first in alphabetical order?

■ cake ☐ fish ☐ tree ☐ paint

Which of these letters are in alphabetical order?

☐ BCFDEG ☐ ZYXWVU ■ JKLMNO ☐ HIJGLK

Which of these words does NOT rhyme with pie?

☐ cry ☐ lie ☐ try ■ field

Which of these words does NOT rhyme with Tim?

☐ slim ☐ trim ■ time ☐ limb

Which of these is a correct sentence?

☐ two hands and two feet ☐ You have two hands and two feet
☐ you have two hands and two feet ■ You have two hands and two feet.

Which word in this sentence is a noun? My house is big.

☐ is ☐ my ☐ big ■ house

Which word in this sentence is a proper noun? My grandparents live in Philadelphia.

☐ my ■ Philadelphia ☐ grandparents ☐ live

Lesson 136

Plurals

A **plural** word is a word that means more than one. For instance, you have one bike, but two bikes. You add an S on to the end to make it plural. Add an S to these words to make them plural.

ball**s**   home**s**

bed**s**   house**s**

brother**s**   school**s**

door**s**   sister**s**

girl**s**   tree**s**

flower**s**   pool**s**

Copywork

Copy these plural words onto the lines below: *bikes stores cars tables friends times*

bikes stores cars
tables friends times

Lesson 137

Plurals

Sometimes a word needs an ES on the end to make it plural. That happens when a word ends with X, SS, SH or CH. Pay attention to the words below and add either an S or an ES to make the word plural.

bucket**s**   bush**es**

church**es**   pencil**s**

brush**es**   torch**es**

princess**es**   prince**s**

fox**es**   flute**s**

dog**s**   cat**s**

Copywork

Copy these plural words onto the lines below: *washes misses brushes peaches wishes taxes*

washes misses brushes
peaches wishes taxes

Lesson 138

Plurals

When a word ends in Y, plurals can be tricky. When there is a vowel before the Y, add an S to make it plural. If there is NOT a vowel before the Y, you change the Y to an I and add ES. Make the following words plural. (When there is not a vowel before the Y, put an X on the Y and then write IES in the blank.)

bab**y̶ ies**   ray**s**

lad**y̶ ies**   fl**y̶ ies**

monkey**s**   boy**s**

cit**y̶ ies**   valley**s**

fami**l̶y̶ ies**   tray**s**

tal**l̶y̶ ies**   trolley**s**

Copywork

Copy these plural words onto the lines below: *toys ways days plays keys*

toys ways days plays
keys

Lesson 139

Plurals

Make the following words plural.

bike**s**   wash**es**

store**s**   bab**ies**

friend**s**   day**s**

miss**es**   time**s**

peach**es**   tax**es**

tr**ies**   way**s**

play**s**   table**s**

brush**es**   wish**es**

Circle the pronouns below.

it   flower   she   they

pencil   her   him   shirt

Lesson 141

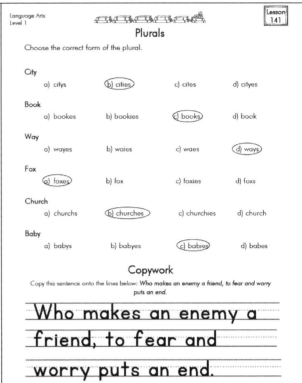

Plurals

Choose the correct form of the plural.

City
   a) citys   **b) cities**   c) cites   d) cityes

Book
   a) bookes   b) bookies   **c) books**   d) book

Way
   a) wayes   b) waies   c) waes   **d) ways**

Fox
   a) foxes   b) fox   c) foxies   d) foxs

Church
   a) churchs   **b) churches**   c) churchies   d) church

Baby
   a) babys   b) babyes   **c) babies**   d) babes

Copywork

Copy this sentence onto the lines below: *Who makes an enemy a friend, to fear and worry puts an end.*

Who makes an enemy a friend, to fear and worry puts an end.

Lesson 142

Matching

Some words just don't follow a rule for plurals. Use the matching game to learn some of the odd forms plurals can take. First, read through the words – the plural is to the right of each word. Then cut out the squares and mix them up, matching the word to its plural. Play it again and again until you are familiar with some of the exceptions to the plural rules!

child	children	mouse	mice
goose	geese	sheep	sheep
cactus	cacti	leaf	leaves

Copywork

Copy this sentence onto the lines below: *There the same thing happened.*

There the same thing happened.

Lesson 143

Matching

Here are some more odd plurals. Again, read through the words first – the plurals are to the right of the words. Then cut them out and mix them up. Add them to your cards from lesson 142 for a bigger challenge!

fish	fish	tooth	teeth
man	men	foot	feet
ox	oxen	person	people

Copywork

Copy this sentence onto the lines below: *A sudden odd surprise made Farmer Brown's boy's hair to rise.*

A sudden odd surprise made Farmer Brown's boy's hair to rise.

Lesson 144

Grammar Review

Circle the nouns and underline the pronouns.

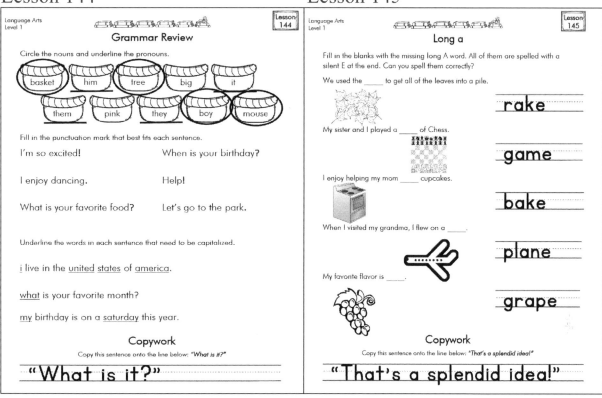

basket, him, tree, big, it, them, pink, they, boy, mouse

Fill in the punctuation mark that best fits each sentence.

I'm so excited!   When is your birthday?

I enjoy dancing.   Help!

What is your favorite food?   Let's go to the park.

Underline the words in each sentence that need to be capitalized.

i live in the united states of america.

what is your favorite month?

my birthday is on a saturday this year.

Copywork

Copy this sentence onto the line below: *"What is it?"*

"What is it?"

Lesson 145

Long a

Fill in the blanks with the missing long A word. All of them are spelled with a silent E at the end. Can you spell them correctly?

We used the _____ to get all of the leaves into a pile.

rake

My sister and I played a _____ of Chess.

game

I enjoy helping my mom _____ cupcakes.

bake

When I visited my grandma, I flew on a _____.

plane

My favorite flavor is _____.

grape

Copywork

Copy this sentence onto the line below: *"That's a splendid idea!"*

"That's a splendid idea!"

Lesson 146

Plurals

Most of the time, when a word ends in F or FE, we change the F or FE to a V and add ES to make the word plural. Rewrite the words below as a plurals in the blanks beside them.

knife **knives**   leaf **leaves**

wolf **wolves**   life **lives**

thief **thieves**   half **halves**

wife **wives**   calf **calves**

loaf **loaves**   shelf **shelves**

elf **elves**   sheaf **sheaves**

Lesson 147

Spelling Word Search

Find the plural words in the puzzle below. Once you find them all, have a parent or sibling read the words to you one at a time while you try to spell them.

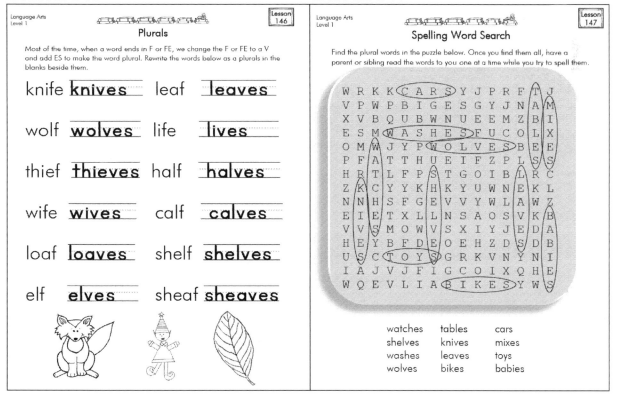

watches   tables   cars
shelves   knives   mixes
washes   leaves   toys
wolves   bikes   babies

89

Lesson 148

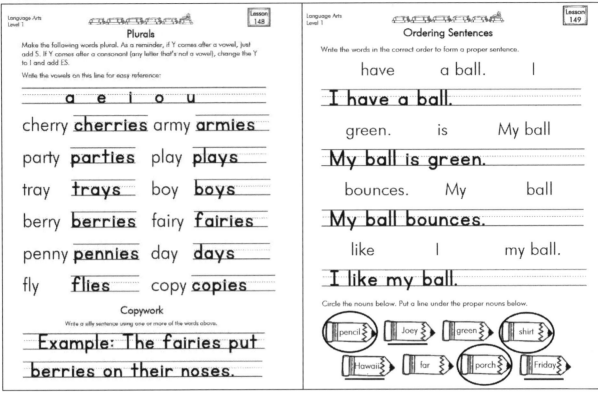

Language Arts
Level 1

Plurals

Make the following words plural. As a reminder, if Y comes after a vowel, just add S. If Y comes after a consonant (any letter that's not a vowel), change the Y to I and add ES.

Write the vowels on this line for easy reference:

a e i o u

cherry **cherries** army **armies**

party **parties** play **plays**

tray **trays** boy **boys**

berry **berries** fairy **fairies**

penny **pennies** day **days**

fly **flies** copy **copies**

Copywork

Write a silly sentence using one or more of the words above.

Example: The fairies put berries on their noses.

Lesson 149

Language Arts
Level 1

Ordering Sentences

Write the words in the correct order to form a proper sentence.

have   a ball.   I

I have a ball.

green.   is   My ball

My ball is green.

bounces.   My   ball

My ball bounces.

like   I   my ball.

I like my ball.

Circle the nouns below. Put a line under the proper nouns below.

pencil   Joey   green   shirt

Hawaii   far   porch   Friday

Lesson 150

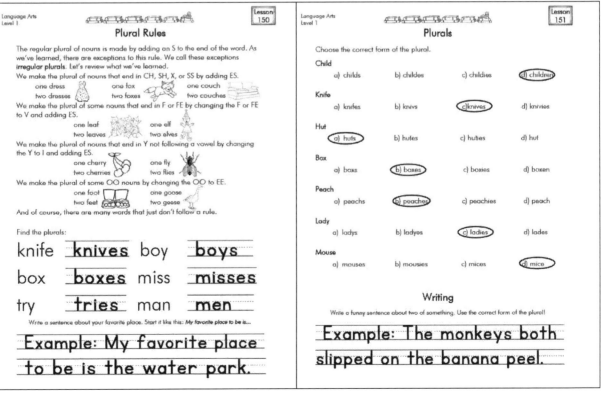

Language Arts
Level 1

Plural Rules

The regular plural of nouns is made by adding an S to the end of the word. As we've learned, there are exceptions to this rule. We call these exceptions **irregular plurals**. Let's review what we've learned.

We make the plural of nouns that end in CH, SH, X, or SS by adding ES.

one dress   one fox   one couch
two dresses   two foxes   two couches

We make the plural of some nouns that end in F or FE by changing the F or FE to V and adding ES.

one leaf   one elf
two leaves   two elves

We make the plural of nouns that end in Y not following a vowel by changing the Y to I and adding ES.

one cherry   one fly
two cherries   two flies

We make the plural of some OO nouns by changing the OO to EE.

one foot   one goose
two feet   two geese

And of course, there are many words that just don't follow a rule.

Find the plurals:

knife **knives** boy **boys**

box **boxes** miss **misses**

try **tries** man **men**

Write a sentence about your favorite place. Start it like this: *My favorite place to be is...*

Example: My favorite place to be is the water park.

Lesson 151

Language Arts
Level 1

Plurals

Choose the correct form of the plural.

Child
  a) childs   b) childes   c) childies   (d) children)

Knife
  a) knifes   b) knivs   (c) knives)   d) knivies

Hut
  (a) huts)   b) hutes   c) huties   d) hut

Box
  a) boxs   (b) boxes)   c) boxies   d) boxen

Peach
  a) peachs   (b) peaches)   c) peachies   d) peach

Lady
  a) ladys   b) ladyes   (c) ladies)   d) lades

Mouse
  a) mouses   b) mousies   c) mices   (d) mice)

Writing

Write a funny sentence about two of something. Use the correct form of the plural!

Example: The monkeys both slipped on the banana peel.

Lesson 152

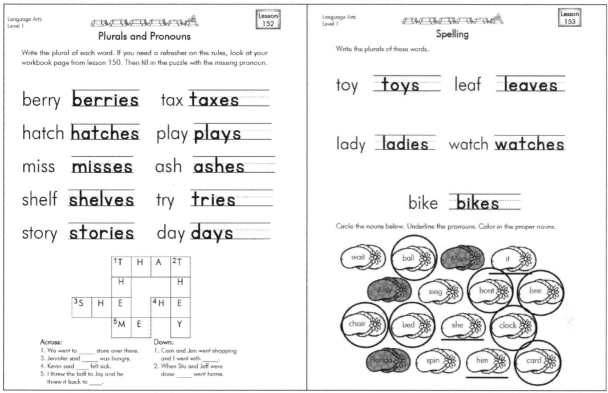

Lesson 153

Lesson 154

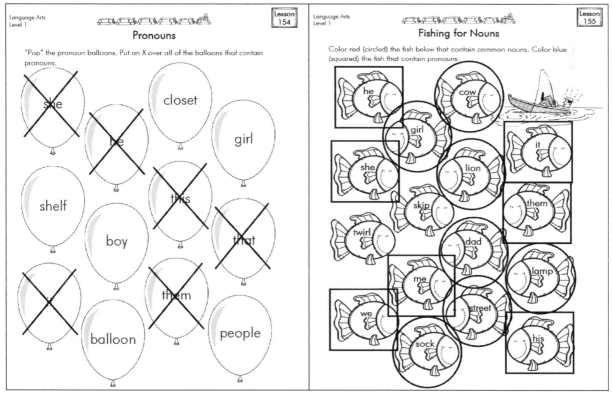

Lesson 155

Lesson 156

Correct the sentences

Correct the sentences below. Remember that all sentences must begin with a capital letter and end with proper punctuation. Proper nouns should be capitalized. Just do your best and learn from any mistakes!

<u>M</u>y favorite day is <u>S</u>unday<u>.</u>

<u>W</u>e are going to the zoo on the first <u>F</u>riday in <u>M</u>ay<u>.</u>

<u>A</u>re you as excited as <u>I</u> am for <u>C</u>hristmas<u>?</u>

<u>I</u>t's freezing in here<u>!</u>

<u>W</u>hat is your favorite color<u>?</u>

<u>I</u> like folding laundry but <u>M</u>om doesn't<u>.</u>   ("Mom" is a name here.)

<u>H</u>ave you met my cousin, <u>J</u>essica<u>?</u>

<u>I</u> love summer<u>!</u>

<u>W</u>inter is my favorite season but my mom likes spring<u>.</u> ("Mom" is not a name here.)

Lesson 157

Plurals

Choose the correct form of the plural. You can find the rules in lesson 150, but remember there are exceptions! Learn from your mistakes if you make them.

One fox, two _____.
  a) foxs   b) foxes ⟲   c) foxies   d) foxen

One leaf, two _____.
  a) leafs   b) leavs   c) leaves ⟲   d) leavies

One lady, two _____.
  a) ladies ⟲   b) ladys   c) ladyes   d) lady

One sheep, two _____.
  a) sheeps   b) sheep ⟲   c) sheepies   d) sheepes

One church, two _____.
  a) churches ⟲   b) churchs   c) churchies   d) church

One ox, two _____.
  a) oxes   b) oxs   c) oxies   d) oxen ⟲

One kiss, two _____.
  a) kisss   b) kissies   c) kissen   d) kisses ⟲

One bird, two _____.
  a) birds ⟲   b) birdes   c) birdies   d) bird

One party, two _____.
  a) partys   b) partes   c) partyes   d) parties ⟲

One toy, two _____.
  a) toyes   b) toyes   c) toys ⟲   d) toy

Lesson 159

Pronouns

Choose the correct pronoun for each sentence. It might help to read the sentence out loud with your choice of pronoun to make sure it sounds right.

I lost my favorite shirt. Can you help _____ find it?
  a) me ⟲   b) my

I love my sister, but sometimes _____ fight.
  a) she   b) we ⟲

Katrina loves stickers. _____ has a whole collection.
  a) She ⟲   b) Her

That ball bounces really high, but _____ bounces higher.
  a) my   b) mine ⟲

James burned _____ finger on the stove.
  a) his ⟲   b) him

Cindy left _____ folder on the counter.
  a) she   b) her ⟲

Our family has two cars, but one of _____ isn't working.
  a) it   b) them ⟲

Lesson 161

Writing

Write a sentence with a name in it. Be sure to capitalize the name! (Example: Liz is my friend.)

(answers will vary)
Ex: Liz is my friend.

Write another sentence, but this time replace the name with a pronoun. (Example: She makes me laugh.)

(answers will vary)
Ex. She makes me laugh.

Pop the pronoun balloons! Put an X over all of the pronouns.

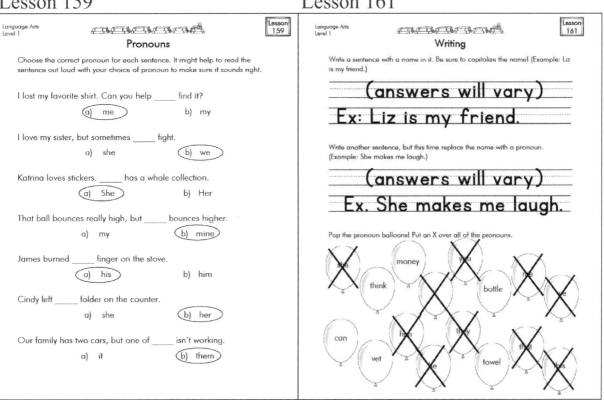

Lesson 162

Capitalization and Punctuation

Choose the proper way to write each sentence.

a. Tim has a cat   b. tim has a cat?   (c.) Tim has a cat.   d. Tim has a cat?

(a.) Jill is a girl.   b. Jill is a girl?   c. jill is a girl?   d. jill is a girl.

a. Maya is happy?   b. maya is happy   (c.) Maya is happy.   d. maya is happy?

a. Is Kiley sad.   b. is Kiley sad?   c. Is Kiley sad   (d.) Is Kiley sad?

a. are you okay.   b. Are you okay.   c. are you okay?   (d.) Are you okay?

(a.) Andy is seven.   b. andy is seven.   c. Andy is seven?   d. Andy is seven

a. is he sleeping?   (b.) Is he sleeping?   c. Is he sleeping.   d. is he sleeping

(a.) Jane is away.   b. Jane is away   c. jane is away?   d. jane is away

Lesson 163

Word Endings

Draw a line from the egg to the right basket. Look at the word endings to help you sort.

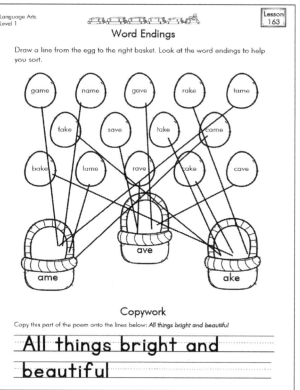

Copywork

Copy this part of the poem onto the lines below: *All things bright and beautiful*

All things bright and beautiful

Lesson 164

Spelling

Choose the letter or letters from the side that best fits the blanks in the word. Each pair is only used once.

n **ai** l

sk **y**

b **oo** k

m **ee** t

b **oa** t

b **u** s

oa
ai
ee
y
u
oo

Copywork

Copy this part of the poem onto the lines below: *All creatures great and small*

All creatures great and small

Lesson 165

Word Builder

Choose the letters from the word box that best fit the blank within the sentences. Then go back through and circle all of the pronouns. These are long a words.

| ale | ain | raid | ai | ay |

(I) fell off (my) bike and have a p**ain** in (my) arm.

(My) brother was sick and (he) looked p**ale**.

(I) need to m**ai**l a letter.

(We) m**ay** go to the park later.

Sometimes (I) am af**raid**.

Copywork

Copy this part of the poem onto the lines below: *All things wise and wonderful*

All things wise and wonderful

Lesson 166

Compound Words

A **compound word** is one word made out of two words. *Bedroom* is one word but it's made from the words *bed* and *room*. Use the words from the box to make compound words out of the words listed.

pot	road	tub	side	set	bone	boat	time

out**side**   sail**boat**

rail**road**   wish**bone**

tea**pot**   bed**time**

sun**set**   bath**tub**

Copywork

Copy this part of the poem onto the lines below: *The Lord God made them all.*

The Lord God made them all.

Lesson 167

Word Endings

Draw a line from the egg to the right basket. Look at the word endings to help you sort.

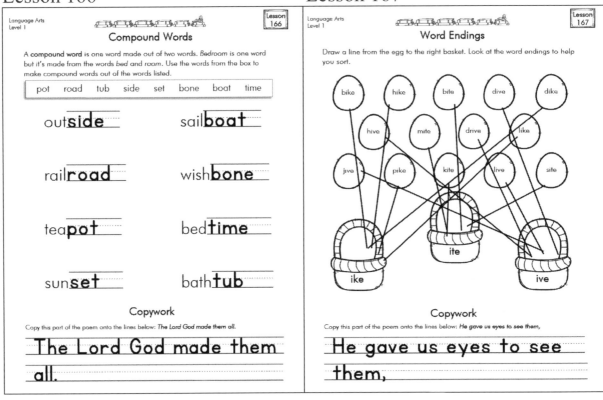

Copywork

Copy this part of the poem onto the lines below: *He gave us eyes to see them,*

He gave us eyes to see them,

Lesson 168

Word Builder

Choose the letters from the box that best fit the blanks within the sentences. Then go back through and circle all of the pronouns. These are long o words.

oat	ow	ode	ad	now	dow

(I) like to bl**ow** bubbles outside.

(I) watched the sn**ow** fall.

(We) r**ode** (our) bikes down the ro**ad**.

The g**oat** ate (my) carrot.

On sunny days (I) see (my) sha**dow**.

Copywork

Copy this part of the poem onto the lines below: *And lips that we might tell*

And lips that we might tell

Lesson 169

Contractions

A **contraction** is two words combined into one. For example, *I am* becomes *I'm* as a contraction. We use an **apostrophe** in place of the letters we take out. Use this matching game to help you learn some contractions and their meanings. First, read through the words – the contraction is to the right of the words it represents. Then cut out the squares and mix them up and try to match them back again.

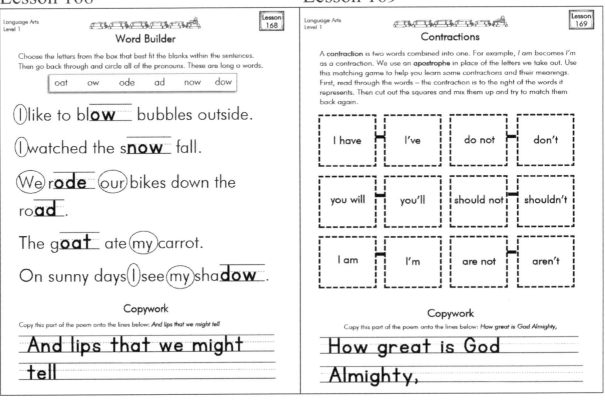

I have	I've	do not	don't
you will	you'll	should not	shouldn't
I am	I'm	are not	aren't

Copywork

Copy this part of the poem onto the lines below: *How great is God Almighty,*

How great is God Almighty,

Lesson 170

Contractions

Find which tree the contraction apple goes to. Remember that the apostrophe represents a missing letter or letters. That can help you figure out the meaning. Draw a line from the apple to the right tree.

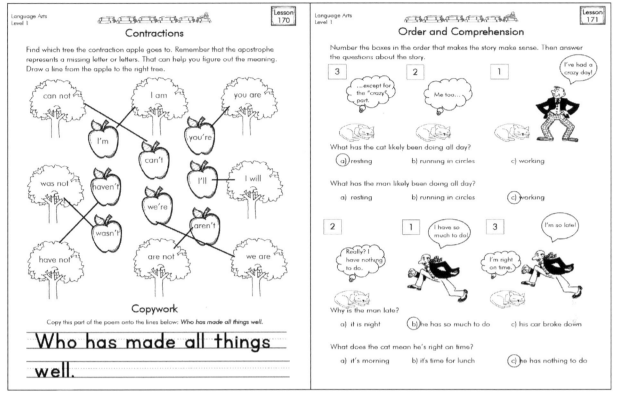

Trees: can not, I am, you are
Apples: I'm, you're, can't
was not, haven't, I'll, I will
we're, wasn't, aren't
have not, are not, we are

Copywork

Copy this part of the poem onto the lines below: *Who has made all things well.*

Who has made all things well.

Lesson 171

Order and Comprehension

Number the boxes in the order that makes the story make sense. Then answer the questions about the story.

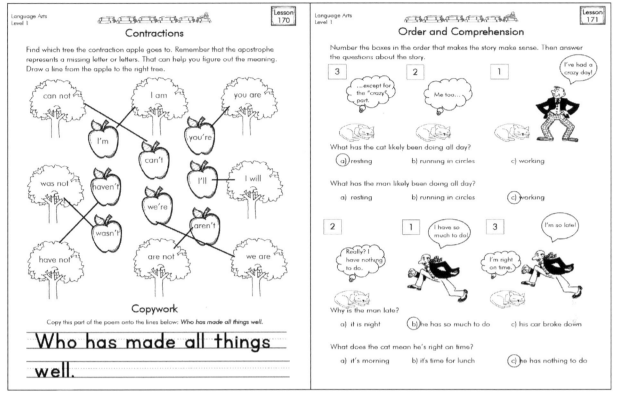

3 — ...except for the "crazy" part.

2 — Me too...

1 — I've had a crazy day!

What has the cat likely been doing all day?
a) resting   b) running in circles   c) working

What has the man likely been doing all day?
a) resting   b) running in circles   c) working

2 — Really? I have nothing to do.

1 — I have so much to do!

3 — I'm right on time!   I'm so late!

Why is the man late?
a) it is night   b) he has so much to do   c) his car broke down

What does the cat mean he's right on time?
a) it's morning   b) it's time for lunch   c) he has nothing to do

Lesson 172

Plurals

Write the plural of each word. If you need a refresher on the rules, look at your workbook page from lesson 150. There are a few tricky ones!

fairy **fairies**   elf **elves**

match **matches**   plot **plots**

kiss **kisses**   sash **sashes**

kite **kites**   try **tries**

pie **pies**   tray **trays**

knife **knives**   tax **taxes**

man **men**   cliff **cliffs**

foot **feet**   wish **wishes**

sheep **sheep**   game **games**

itch **itches**   mouse **mice**

Lesson 173

Noun Review

Do you remember the different kinds of nouns? Color red (circled) the common nouns. Color blue (squared) the proper nouns. Color green (triangled) the pronouns. Every flower should be colored!

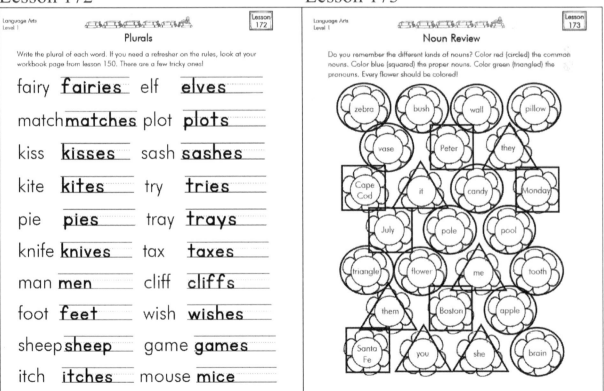

Words in flowers: zebra, bush, wall, pillow, vase, Peter, they, Cape Cod, it, candy, Monday, July, pole, pool, triangle, flower, me, tooth, them, Boston, apple, Santa Fe, you, she, brain

Lesson 174

My Character

Draw a character of some kind. It can be anything you want. It can be silly, have any job, or not even be human – anything you want. Be creative!

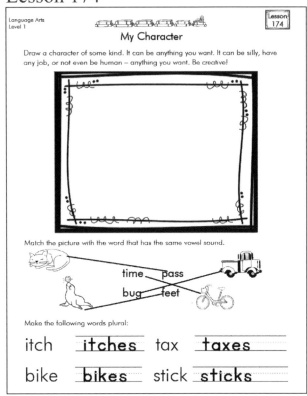

Match the picture with the word that has the same vowel sound.

time   pass

bug   feet

Make the following words plural:

itch   **itches**   tax   **taxes**

bike   **bikes**   stick   **sticks**

We hope you had a great year with EP Language Arts 1.

EP provides free, complete, high quality online homeschool curriculum for children around the world. Find more of our courses and resources on our site, allinonehomeschool.com.

If you prefer offline materials, consider Genesis Curriculum which takes a book of the Bible and turns it into daily lessons in science, social studies, and language arts for your children to learn all together. The curriculum also includes learning Biblical languages. Genesis Curriculum offers Rainbow Readers and a new math curriculum which is also done all together and is based on each day's Bible reading. GC Steps is an offline preschool and kindergarten program. Learn more about our expanding curriculum on our site, GenesisCurriculum.com.

Made in the USA
Middletown, DE
10 July 2023

34841860R00057